First published in the United States of America in 2000 by
Rizzoli International Publications, Inc.
300 Park Avenue South, New York, NY 10010

© Rosalyn Dexter 1999

Rosalyn Dexter has asserted her right to be identified as the author of this
work in accordance with the Copyright, Design and Patents Act, 1988.

First published in the United Kingdom im 1999 by Ebury Press
20 Vauxhall Bridge Road, London SW1V 2SA

ISBN 0-8478-2265-8

Library of Congress Catalog Card Number is available upon request

Printed and bound by Graphicom, Italy

Book design, layout, illustration and paintings by Rosalyn Dexter

Many thanks to all my dear friends who supported me through the life
challenges of the last three years while I wrote this. Thanks to Amelia Thorpe
and Denise Bates at Ebury Press for their leap of faith and Martin and Terry
for leading me to them, and to Isambard Thomas for his patience.

To Mum and Dad, Bernard and Mal, Ann, Jonny and Selwyn

So many silver linings
The clouds are truly rich

Thank you

The publisher thanks the following people and organizations for their
permission to reproduce the photographs in the book: pp8-9, 60-1
photographs by Armando Salas Portugal, Barragan Foundation – Switzerland;
pp10-11 Richard Bryant/Arcaid; pp12-13 Koshino House/Tadao Ando
Architect & Associates; pp 16-17 photograph by Robert F. Mates © The
Solomon R. Guggenheim Foundation, New York; p25 Photonica/Kerama; p90
The Image Bank/Archive Photos; p96 Architectural Association/Osman Vlora;
p99 Richard Glover; p145 Telegraph Colour Library

内容

WE SHAPE OUR BUILDINGS,

THEREAFTER THEY SHAPE US

Winston Churchill

INNER

内

MACROCOSM ... OUR OUTER WORLD BEING A REFLECTION OF OUR

INNER WORLD ... AND VICE VERSA

OUTER

外

SUGGESTING

THAT OUR ENVIRONMENT AFFECTS US MORE THAN WE REALIZE

SEEN AND UNSEEN

FENG SHUI
IS ABOUT BALANCE
IN ALL THINGS

AND

BRINGING

THAT AWARE

TO DESIGN

FENG SHUI IS THE VITAL ELEMENT THAT CAN MAKE

CONCERNED WITH ENHANCING OUR CHOICES

NOT CONDEMNING THEM

GOOD DESIGN GREAT!

... AT MORE LEVELS THAN WE REALIZE

ADDING ANOTHER DIMENSION TO DESIGN

A FEEL-GOOD FACTOR

YOU KNOW HOW YOU FEEL GOOD AT ONE TABLE
IN A RESTAURANT ... AND NOT AT ANOTHER ...

YOU WORK WELL AT ONE DESK ... NOT AT ANOTHER

SOMEONE ELSE IS COMFORTABLE
WHERE YOU ARE NOT!

YOUR INSTINCTS MOVE YOU TO A PLACE OF
MORE COMFORT ...

... MORE EASE.

WHEN YOU ARE MORE AT EASE
YOU FEEL MORE SECURE
FEELING MORE SECURE ALLOWS YOU TO HAVE
A GREATER SENSE OF PERSONAL POWER

POWER THROUGH DESIGN

■

WHAT A CONCEPT

中文耳語 風水

No,

it is not about rearranging your sofas to change your life,

although it is a bit like decorating with a sixth sense

and can be the ultimate environmental design.

Phonetically pronounced "Foong Schwiy"[1] or "Fung Schoy,"[2]

Feng Shui is a flexible combination of art and science –

albeit a science which is not yet fully understood and that

goes back over 4,000 years to the dawn of Chinese civilization.

1 Mandarin – northern China.
2 Cantonese – southern China.

The words Feng Shui literally mean wind 風 and water 水,

representing the traditional Chinese concept of man

harmonizing with his environment.

All matter has vibration – the Hindus call it Prana –

the Hebrews call it Ruach – the Greeks call it Pneuma –

the Japanese call it Ki and the Chinese call it Chi.

Chi roughly translates as the life force or cosmic breath

which pervades all of life. It is the force of change and

transformation that is believed to have created the

landscapes of our planet.

If we consider Chi to be a current of energy, when we are out of step with the natural flow, it is against this current that we struggle – *literally*. Feng Shui is concerned with overcoming this struggle by harnessing supportive Chi – via placement – design – element – color – and much more.

RESTORING THE NATURAL FLOW

We all know the impact the moon has on the tides of the ocean, which is an enormous body of water. Well, we are over 60% water, so what impact might the moon have on us? Less well known is the fact that some surgeons are cautious about performing surgery around the time of the full moon because of the impact on the flow of the blood in the body.

It would seem that mankind and the planet are much more connected than we realize.

A BUTTERFLY FLAPS ITS WINGS IN THE INDIAN OCEAN AND A BREEZE BLOWS IN THE PACIFIC

EVERYTHING IS CONNECTED

了解

UNDERSTANDING THIS INTERACTIVE BALANCE

IS THE HEART OF FENG SHUI

風水中心

和諧

HEAVEN

HARMONY

EARTH

道路

THE

WAY

THE STORY OF THE TURTLE 龜故事

The story goes that the great sage and first ruler of China, Fu Hsi, was sitting by the banks of the Lo River, meditating, when a turtle emerged from the water. While observing the turtle, he noticed an unusual pattern of black and white markings on its shell. Their symmetry intrigued him, as the markings numerically added up to 15 in all directions.

IN A FLASH OF DIVINE INSPIRATION –

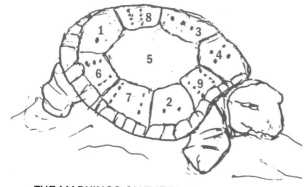

THE MARKINGS ON THE TURTLE
The turtle represents protection, longevity, and wisdom.

4	9	2
3	5	7
8	1	6

The numbers add up to 15 in any direction.

THE WORKINGS OF THE UNIVERSE WERE REVEALED TO HIM!

This revelation of Fu Hsi's was not too dissimilar to the moment

Einstein awoke from his dream with the formula for the theory of

relativity. It took science years to accept Einstein's hypothesis –

for it had taken a revolutionary quantum leap beyond the known.

ARE WE NOW WILLING TO LEAP BEYOND THE KNOWN?

THERE ARE MANY ILLUSIONS IN LIFE

AT THIS MOMENT – YOU MAY THINK THAT YOU
ARE SITTING STILL, BUT YOU AND THE PLANET
ARE CAREERING THROUGH SPACE
AT OVER 30,000 MILES PER HOUR.

IF IT WERE NOT FOR COLUMBUS,

幻影

WE WOULD BELIEVE OUR PLANET WAS FLAT

LOGIC DOESN'T SEEM TO ALWAYS GET IT RIGHT

SUGGESTING THAT THE MIND

THOUGH IT MAY BE A GREAT SERVANT

IS A RATHER LIMITED MASTER

古

ALLOW THAT WHICH THE MIND MAY RESIST

THE UNKNOWN

THE NEW

THE ANCIENT

SPEAKING OF ANCIENT ...

BACK THEN

Feng Shui practitioners were employed by the emperor to determine the best burial sites for their ancestors. It was believed that being buried in harmony with the elements of nature would have a direct and beneficial effect on the well-being of their descendants.

As this science evolved, Feng Shui advice was sought for all kinds of buildings and even eventually for whole cities.

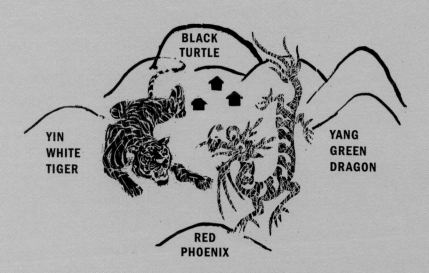

The Form School describes this union of the Yin White Tiger and the Yang Green Dragon – where they meet is considered to be the most auspicious location. If the hills continue one behind the other, this was considered even more auspicious as it was symbolic of their mating. The Yin White Tiger, the Yang Green Dragon, the Red Phoenix, and Black Turtle are called the Celestial Animals.

THERE ARE TWO TRADITIONAL SCHOOLS OF FENG SHUI

The first is the Form School, which is based on the contours of the landscape and its waterways in relation to a site or building. Its references are shrouded in symbolic representations of Celestial Animals, the elements, and the intangible forces of Yin and Yang. This method requires a great deal of intuitive insight.

The second method, which developed alongside this, was the Compass School. By contrast, this method assigns less importance to the form of the landscape – adopting a more mathematical approach. Heavily grounded in the *I Ching* and its eight Trigrams,[1] it uses the Chinese horoscope and numerology. The belief was that honing the analysis to a more personal level, by taking into account the influence the planets had on the quality of the location and you, allowed your personal Chi to be harmoniously aligned with the Chi of the environment.

These two schools began to merge by the early twentieth century, resulting in the method popular today in the East and West, and which this book presents.

1 *I Ching* (see page 44)

YIN

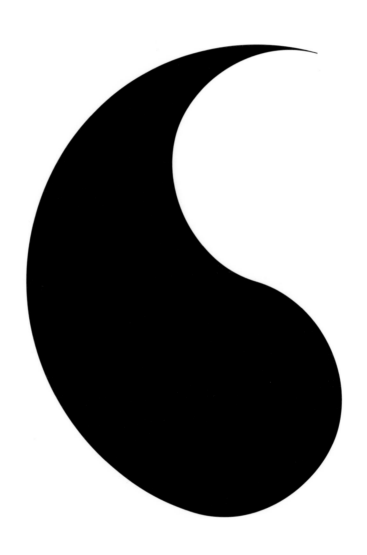

陰

YANG

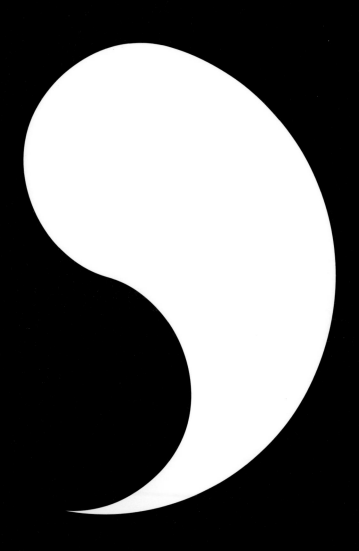

YIN AND YANG IS THE DYNAMIC UNDERLYING FENG SHUI AND ALL CHINESE PHILOSOPHY

Two forces complementing and opposing each other –

shaping our world – and everything in it.

陽是活躍的　　YANG IS ACTIVE

陰是被動的　　YIN IS RESTFUL

THE BELIEF IS ... Yang energy emanates from the Heavens, descending from above – controlling our morality ... Yin energy ascends from the earth – controlling our desires and choices

YANG DESCENDS, BECOMING
MORE CONCENTRATED –
FASTER – HARDER AND HOTTER

YIN RISES AND DIFFUSES,
BECOMING SLOWER
AND COOLER

Male	Female
Hot	Cold
Movement	Stillness
Sun	Moon
Centripetal	Centrifugal
Contract	Expand
White	Black
Even numbers	Odd numbers
Positive	Negative
Light	Dark

Without darkness there is no light   Without stillness there is no movement

YIN WITHIN YANG ... YANG WITHIN YIN

YIN AND YANG ARE INSEPARABLE

THE PERFECT BALANCE

represented in this symbol of unity

THE CYCLE OF LIFE AND DEATH

ONE OF THE WORLD'S MOST INFLUENTIAL

完美的平衡

NEWSPAPERS, "THE FINANCIAL TIMES"

chose PINK,

a feminine color – YIN,

to write about commercial data – YANG.

FENG SHUI WOULD SUGGEST

YIN – YANG

PERFECT BALANCE

APPLYING FENG SHUI

Thousands of years ago – long before Einstein's theory – Fu Hsi and his followers proposed that matter and energy were interchangeable. The proposal was that the Universe comprised MATTER – ENERGY – CHI

which were presented as the five basic elements believed to be the basis for all living things: WOOD – FIRE – EARTH – METAL – WATER

These elements were considered incredibly potent forces that were continually interacting with each other in what were called THE FIVE STAGES OF CHANGE.

As illustrated in this star cycle.

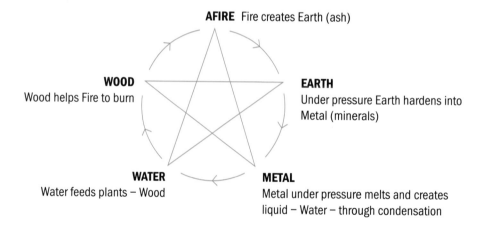

AFIRE Fire creates Earth (ash)

WOOD
Wood helps Fire to burn

EARTH
Under pressure Earth hardens into Metal (minerals)

WATER
Water feeds plants – Wood

METAL
Metal under pressure melts and creates liquid – Water – through condensation

When the Sages were working with these Five Stages of Change and the laws of Yin and Yang, they were also interested in numerology and codifying information. They believed the Universe was based on mathematical principles and that these numbers were a kind of key that could unlock a hidden wisdom which would enable them to harness the invisible forces that govern the balance between heaven and earth.

They ascribed numerical value to each stage of transformation.

FIRE – 9   EARTH – 2, 5, 8   METAL – 6, 7   WATER – 1   WOOD – 3, 4

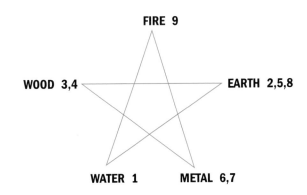

THESE FIVE STAGES OF CHANGE RELATE TO EACH OTHER ACCORDING
TO CYCLES, WHICH ARE EXPLAINED IN MORE DETAIL ON PAGE 148.

Using the star cycle and observing the subtle changes in the electromagnetic forces around them, the Ancient Sages were able to ascribe certain qualities and life aspirations to each of the eight compass locations represented by the eight Trigrams of the octagonal Pa Kua.[1]

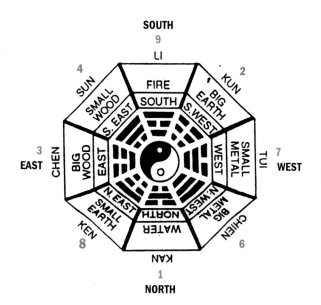

PA KUA: Pa means 8, Kua means Trigrams.

The Yin odd numbers have the cardinal points (North, South, East, and West)
The Yang even numbers have the secondary positions.
This is the Yang arrangement of Trigrams used for living environments.
The Yin arrangement is most often used for burial sites.

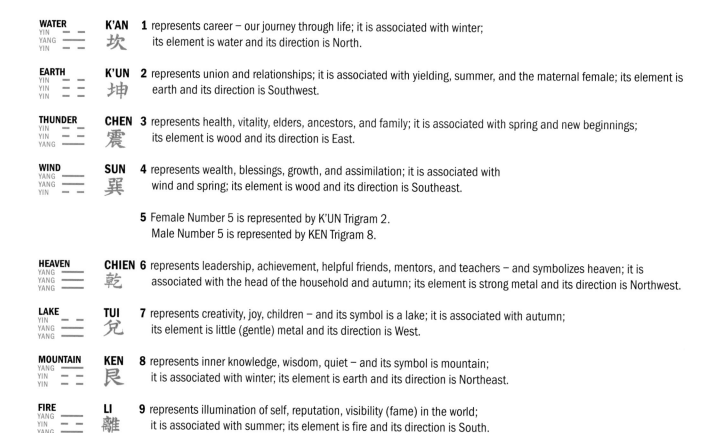

WATER K'AN **1** represents career – our journey through life; it is associated with winter; its element is water and its direction is North.

EARTH K'UN **2** represents union and relationships; it is associated with yielding, summer, and the maternal female; its element is earth and its direction is Southwest.

THUNDER CHEN **3** represents health, vitality, elders, ancestors, and family; it is associated with spring and new beginnings; its element is wood and its direction is East.

WIND SUN **4** represents wealth, blessings, growth, and assimilation; it is associated with wind and spring; its element is wood and its direction is Southeast.

5 Female Number 5 is represented by K'UN Trigram 2.
Male Number 5 is represented by KEN Trigram 8.

HEAVEN CHIEN **6** represents leadership, achievement, helpful friends, mentors, and teachers – and symbolizes heaven; it is associated with the head of the household and autumn; its element is strong metal and its direction is Northwest.

LAKE TUI **7** represents creativity, joy, children – and its symbol is a lake; it is associated with autumn; its element is little (gentle) metal and its direction is West.

MOUNTAIN KEN **8** represents inner knowledge, wisdom, quiet – and its symbol is mountain; it is associated with winter; its element is earth and its direction is Northeast.

FIRE LI **9** represents illumination of self, reputation, visibility (fame) in the world; it is associated with summer; its element is fire and its direction is South.

1 Fu Hsi's work uncovered these eight Trigrams that represent the secret of life and supposedly contain the wisdom of the Universe – the resulting 64 Hexagrams of the *I Ching* - The Book of Change – an oracle of profound wisdom that was intended as a guide along one's path in life. The texts of the 64 hexagrams represents all possible stages of change in the individual – from birth to death. It formed the foundation for the Philosophical movement, Chinese divination, astrology, and Feng Shui.

To apply this information for Feng Shui, we use the Lo Shu numbered grid, named after the River Lo. This grid was inspired by the markings on the back of the turtle all those years ago. The significant aspects of the Trigrams relate to the compass directions and their corresponding numbers on this grid. The grid is divided into nine numbered sections which form either a rectangle or square. Each of the numbers on the grid represents a compass point location corresponding to the Pa Kua.

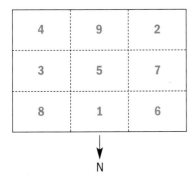

4	9	2
3	5	7
8	1	6

N

1 = NORTH, 2 = SOUTHWEST, 3 = EAST,

4 = SOUTHEAST, 5 = CENTER, 6 = NORTHWEST,

7 = WEST, 8 = NORTHEAST, 9 = SOUTH.

5 is always in the CENTER (except in Time Dimension Feng Shui[2]).

This flexible grid is applied to a whole site − a building − or to an individual room within a building and even shrinks to work on a surface as small as your desk. So a complete site, its garden, or simply a room within a building can be analyzed.

In Ancient China they believed that the place they occupied on the Earth was the Middle Kingdom and since for them the sun's maximum heat and light came from the South, they aligned the Pa Kua for Li to represent the heat of the South. Traditionalists within Feng Shui believe that the Trigrams stay the same for the Southern Hemisphere when the sun's main heat is in the North. Another school of thought is discussed on page 156.

2 Time Dimension Feng Shui is an advanced form of practice and its teachings require a deep understanding of the basics of Feng Shui. It is better suited to a classroom situation where you can interact and ask questions.

To apply this information, draw a layout of your environment and superimpose the grid, aligning the numbers of the grid with the orientation of your building using a compass.

North of the building = 1
Southwest of the building = 2

SOUTHEAST 4	SOUTH 9	SOUTHWEST 2
EAST 3	5	WEST 7
NORTHEAST 8	NORTH 1	NORTHWEST 6

N

If your building has an irregular shape — i.e. not square or rectangular, as are ideal — then place the main body of the building within the grid and mark the compass directions (refer to the information on negative and positive space given on page 152).

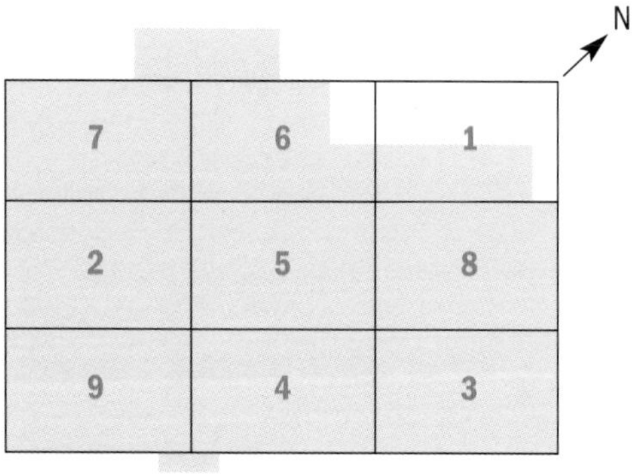

N

7	6	1
2	5	8
9	4	3

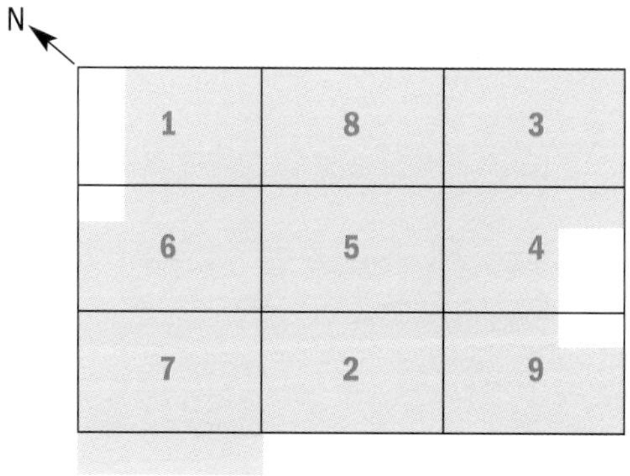

N

1	8	3
6	5	4
7	2	9

If there are different levels to the building, each succeeding floor is similarly divided into nine sections.

In simplistic terms, 4 is represented in the Southeast and that is about success – wealth – treasures – its element is wood and its color green; 9 is represented in the South and that is about fame, and its element is fire and its color is red.

SOUTHEAST WOOD 4 GREEN, PALE BLUE WEALTH – BLESSINGS	SOUTH FIRE 9 RED FAME	SOUTHWEST EARTH 2 YELLOWS RELATIONSHIPS
EAST WOOD 3 GREEN, PALE BLUE ANCESTORS	EARTH 5 YELLOWS, ORANGE CHI – HEALTH	WEST METAL 7 WHITE, GOLD, SILVER, GRAY CREATIVITY
NORTHEAST EARTH 8 YELLOWS, ORANGE, BROWN KNOWLEDGE	NORTH WATER 1 NAVY/BLUE CAREER	NORTHWEST METAL 6 WHITE, GOLD, SILVER, GRAY HELPFUL FRIENDS

In addition to representing an element and color, these sections are also represented by shapes and symbolic images – these are called cures and are used by practitioners to balance and enhance an environment (for more information see page 151).

The Chinese compass – THE LUO PAN – is a reference compass illustrated with symbols that indicate good or bad Feng Shui. The traditional presentation on the Luo Pan displays South at the top and North at the bottom – this still refers to magnetic North as on Western compasses.

COMPASS READING

Various electrical appliances and objects made of steel or iron can distort the compass readings, so walk around the building holding the compass steady until a reading is consistent in several parts of the building, then apply this reading to the grid.

呼吸

哲學

INTUITIVE DISCOVERY

4,000 YEARS OLD

64 HEXAGRAMS

REPRESENTING

ALL POSSIBLE STAGES OF CHANGE

FROM BIRTH TO DEATH

科學

SCIENTIFIC DISCOVERY

40 YEARS OLD
64 CODONS OF DNA
GENETIC CODE
FOR LIFE!

YOUR PREFERRED COMPASS DIRECTIONS

In our Western culture it is common to say the cardinal points in the following order: NORTH, SOUTH, EAST, WEST. But the Chinese follow the cycle of the sun and say: EAST, SOUTH, WEST, NORTH – sunrise through to sunset – its natural cycle!

HARNESSING YOUR PREFERRED COMPASS DIRECTIONS AND LOCATIONS IS THE CORNERSTONE OF TRADITIONAL FENG SHUI.

With the knowledge of your best compass directions and the cures, you can manipulate a difficult building situation into one that supports you, or – even better – choose one that is good for you to start with.

So ... now that you know how to apply the grid for analysis to your building it is time to be informed about your personal best directions. Harnessing your best directions maximizes the potential of Feng Shui to create more balance, joy, and success in your life.

There are three important directions.

These are: The direction the energy is coming from as it enters your front door; the direction the energy is coming from as it enters the back of your oven; and, when you are sleeping, the direction the energy is coming from as it enters the crown of your head.

These are called the three power points: MIND – BODY – SPIRIT.

The energy coming in through the door feeds the MIND,[1] the oven feeds the BODY, and the energy coming in through the crown of the head feeds the SPIRIT.

Harnessing one of these is good – harnessing two is very good – being able to harness all three is excellent.

思想
MIND

身體
BODY

心靈
SPIRIT

[1] The direction you face when you work/study is considered "mind" energy.

ASCERTAINING YOUR PREFERRED COMPASS DIRECTIONS

To ascertain your personal preferred directions and locations, use the chart opposite to establish your Kua Number. (Kua means Trigram – from Pa Kua.) Despite being born in the same year, you will notice that males and females have different Kua Numbers. This is because Chinese philosophy views them as opposites.

The male number is based on the Yang (contracting – descending) chart.
The female number is based on the Yin (expanding – ascending) chart.

Based on the lunar calendar, the Chinese New Year occurs between mid-January and mid-February falling on the 2nd new moon after the winter solstice.
So, in a given year – if your date of birth comes before the Chinese New Year look to the prior year for your Kua Number.

For example – if your date of birth is February 18, 1939 – your birth year is calculated as 1938 as the new year starts on February 19, 1939.

Your Chinese Animal and Element are listed in the following chart alongside your Kua Number (more information is given on page 81).

YEAR OF BIRTH	NEW YEAR STARTS	KUA NUMBER MALE	FEMALE	ANIMAL	ELEMENT	YEAR OF BIRTH	NEW YEAR STARTS	KUA NUMBER MALE	FEMALE	ANIMAL	ELEMENT
1928	JAN 23	9	6	DRAGON	EARTH	1968	JAN 31	5	1	MONKEY	EARTH
1929	FEB 10	8	7	SNAKE	EARTH	1969	FEB 17	4	2	ROOSTER	EARTH
1930	JAN 30	7	8	HORSE	METAL	1970	FEB 6	3	3	DOG	METAL
1931	FEB 17	6	9	SHEEP	METAL	1971	JAN 27	2	4	PIG	METAL
1932	FEB 6	5	1	MONKEY	WATER	1972	JAN 16	1	5	RAT	WATER
1933	JAN 26	4	2	ROOSTER	WATER	1973	JAN 3	9	6	OX	WATER
1934	FEB 14	3	3	DOG	WOOD	1974	JAN 23	8	7	TIGER	WOOD
1935	FEB 4	2	4	PIG	WOOD	1975	FEB 11	7	8	RABBIT	WOOD
1936	JAN 24	1	5	RAT	FIRE	1976	JAN 31	6	9	DRAGON	FIRE
1937	FEB 11	9	6	OX	FIRE	1977	FEB 18	5	1	SNAKE	FIRE
1938	JAN 31	8	7	TIGER	EARTH	1978	FEB 7	4	2	HORSE	EARTH
1939	FEB 19	7	8	RABBIT	EARTH	1979	JAN 28	3	3	SHEEP	EARTH
1940	FEB 8	6	9	DRAGON	METAL	1980	FEB 16	2	4	MONKEY	METAL
1941	JAN 27	5	1	SNAKE	METAL	1981	FEB 5	1	5	ROOSTER	METAL
1942	FEB 15	4	2	HORSE	WATER	1982	JAN 25	9	6	DOG	WATER
1943	FEB 5	3	3	SHEEP	WATER	1983	FEB 13	8	7	PIG	WATER
1944	JAN 25	2	4	MONKEY	WOOD	1984	FEB 2	7	8	RAT	WOOD
1945	JAN 13	1	5	ROOSTER	WOOD	1985	FEB 20	6	9	OX	WOOD
1946	FEB 2	9	6	DOG	FIRE	1986	FEB 9	5	1	TIGER	FIRE
1947	JAN 22	8	7	PIG	FIRE	1987	JAN 29	4	2	RABBIT	FIRE
1948	FEB 10	7	8	RAT	EARTH	1988	FEB 17	3	3	DRAGON	EARTH
1949	JAN 29	6	9	OX	EARTH	1989	FEB 6	2	4	SNAKE	EARTH
1950	FEB 17	5	1	TIGER	METAL	1990	JAN 27	1	5	HORSE	METAL
1951	FEB 6	4	2	RABBIT	METAL	1991	FEB 15	9	6	SHEEP	METAL
1952	JAN 27	3	3	DRAGON	WATER	1992	FEB 4	8	7	MONKEY	WATER
1953	JAN 14	2	4	SNAKE	WATER	1993	JAN 23	7	8	ROOSTER	WATER
1954	FEB 3	1	5	HORSE	WOOD	1994	FEB 10	6	9	DOG	WOOD
1955	JAN 24	9	6	SHEEP	WOOD	1995	JAN 31	5	1	PIG	WOOD
1956	JAN 12	8	7	MONKEY	FIRE	1996	FEB 19	4	2	RAT	FIRE
1957	JAN 31	7	8	ROOSTER	FIRE	1997	FEB 7	3	3	OX	FIRE
1958	FEB 18	6	9	DOG	EARTH	1998	JAN 28	2	4	TIGER	EARTH
1959	FEB 8	5	1	PIG	EARTH	1999	FEB 16	1	5	RABBIT	EARTH
1960	JAN 28	4	2	RAT	METAL	2000	FEB 5	9	6	DRAGON	METAL
1961	FEB 15	3	3	OX	METAL	2001	JAN 24	8	7	SNAKE	METAL
1962	FEB 5	2	4	TIGER	WATER	2002	FEB 12	7	8	HORSE	WATER
1963	JAN 25	1	5	RABBIT	WATER	2003	FEB 1	6	9	SHEEP	WATER
1964	FEB 1	9	6	DRAGON	WOOD	2004	JAN 22	5	1	MONKEY	WOOD
1965	FEB 2	8	7	SNAKE	WOOD	2005	FEB 9	4	2	ROOSTER	WOOD
1966	JAN 21	7	8	HORSE	FIRE	2006	JAN 29	3	3	DOG	FIRE
1967	FEB 9	6	9	SHEEP	FIRE	2007	FEB 18	2	4	PIG	FIRE

Kua numbers and animal signs/elements can be calculated well into the millennium by simply following the repetition of the cycles.

Having ascertained your Kua Number, identify your personal preferred directions in the following chart. Locate your Kua Number along the top – your preferred order of compass directions are then listed in descending order starting with the best.

DIRECTION IS THE **WAY** YOU ARE FACING OR SLEEPING.
LOCATION IS THE **PLACE** WHERE YOU ARE SITTING OR SLEEPING.

	M/F	M/F	M/F	M/F	M	F	M/F	M/F	M/F	M/F
Direction	1	2	3	4	5	5	6	7	8	9
1st	SE	NE	S	N	NE	SW	W	NW	SW	E
2nd	E	W	N	S	W	NW	NE	SW	NW	SE
3rd	S	NW	SE	E	NW	W	SW	NE	W	N
4th	N	SW	E	SE	SW	NE	NW	W	NE	S
5th	W	E	SW	NW	E	S	SE	N	S	NE
6th	NE	SE	NW	SW	SE	N	E	S	N	W
7th	NW	S	NE	W	S	E	N	SE	E	SW
8th	SW	N	W	NE	N	SE	S	E	SE	NW

M = male   F= female

The first four directions bring slightly different kinds of luck.

The 1st is success, good for sleeping, and sitting at your desk – main front door – master bedroom.

The 2nd is health and relates to dining room and oven placement.

The 3rd is family harmony, especially good for bed orientation.

The 4th is for general good luck, protection, and clarity; and good for a study or a child's bed.

The last four directions are not as supportive and can create variably blame, chaos, sabotage, and laziness – but they are good locations for positioning the toilet and kitchen.

北
東
南
西

According to the Compass School of Feng Shui, mankind is divided into two groups: people whose Kua Numbers are 1, 3, 4, or 9 (the Chinese call this the East Group of numbers) and people whose Kua Numbers are 2, 5, 8, 6, or 7 (the West Group of numbers). These groups do not apply to any cultural differences – people from the same group are more compatible with each other only in that they have the same four preferred sleeping and door directions – though in a varying order.

It is not always possible to utilize only your best directions and locations – and harnessing these becomes even more complicated when members of a household belong to different groups. So – in a partnership situation – if you are from different groups, compromise is the solution. The female chooses the better sleeping position – the male his preferred front door location and if possible the oven placement (provider) – or vice versa if the female is the bigger bread winner.

In terms of location and direction, the East and West Groups may have different needs. But in terms of compatibility – romantic and professional – they can share great passion and friendship with each other (see compatibility page 78).[1]

[1] Compensating for nonsupportive directions is explained in more detail on page 148.

三個一組

THE CHINESE TRADITIONALLY BELIEVE

HEAVEN LUCK   (fate)

EARTH LUCK   which can be

MAN LUCK   helping to

DO NOT UNDERESTIMATE THE RESULTS

THAT THERE ARE THREE KINDS OF LUCK

IN OUR JOURNEY THROUGH LIFE

improved via Feng Shui – which in turn gives support to our

nurture us through challenging times.

OF PRACTICING FENG SHUI.

IT CAN TRULY ENHANCE YOUR LIFE.

OUR ENVIRONMENT

IS MORE

THAN IT SEEMS

SO ARE WE

TALKING OF WE

LET'S TAKE A CLOSER LOOK

AT

RELATIONSHIPS

AND

COMPATIBILITY

■

PERSONAL

AND

PROFESSIONAL

PERSONALITY ANALYSIS

For personality analysis, there are three numbers you must calculate.

友誼

The 1st number reveals your Basic Nature – it is active during your first seven years, and then again in your late twenties – early thirties – and on, gently influencing you in the interim years.

The 2nd – your Personality Number – reveals your adaptive qualities and is active from seven years old to your late twenties.

The 3rd – your Journey Number – reveals your attitudes and behavior and represents your most satisfying path in life.

All of these numbers combined create "the wholeness" of who you are. The character traits relating to your 1st number, though strong, are only part of the story.

The belief is that you function under the influence of your 1st number until the age of seven, at which point your 2nd number, your Personality Number, kicks in, influencing your continuing experiences. This 2nd number is your adaptive behavioral presentation in the world – influenced externally by environment – family – lifestyle – geography, etc., with your 1st number (Basic Nature) basking in the background. Then in your late twenties – early thirties – your 1st number resurrects itself, taking control and leading you on into your more mature future.
(There are parallels here with the Western version of mid-life crisis).

Simultaneously during the above, your 3rd number – your Journey Number – is gently whispering to you … ever endeavoring to guide you along the path that is most satisfying for you personally – helping you weave a path through life's challenges – always influenced by your 1st and 2nd numbers.

YOUR JOURNEY NUMBER IS THAT INNER VOICE GUIDING YOU

WHEN APPARENT LIFE CHOICES SHOW UP.

YOUR BASIC NATURE NUMBER

For personality analysis we use Chiu Kung Ming Li astrology, which is based on the solar calendar. This is calculated by the movement of the Earth around the sun, as opposed to the lunar calendar which is based on the moon as it orbits the Earth. The year for this solar calendar begins on February 4, which represents the halfway point between the Winter Solstice and Spring Equinox.

Looking at the chart below you will find your Basic Nature Number, next to your year of birth. This first number is used to determine your other numbers for personality analysis. If in a given year your date of birth comes before February 4 look to the prior year for your Basic Nature Number.

For example, if your date of birth is February 3, 1951, your Basic Nature Number is calculated for 1950, i.e. 5 for males – 1 for females.
Most of you will note that this number is the same as your Kua Number except for those born around the time of the Chinese New Year.

Year of birth	Basic Nature Number Male	Female	Year of birth	Basic Nature Number Male	Female	Year of birth	Basic Nature Number Male	Female
1928	9	6	1955	9	6	1982	9	6
1929	8	7	1956	8	7	1983	8	7
1930	7	8	1957	7	8	1984	7	8
1931	6	9	1958	6	9	1985	6	9
1932	5	1	1959	5	1	1986	5	1
1933	4	2	1960	4	2	1987	4	2
1934	3	3	1961	3	3	1988	3	3
1935	2	4	1962	2	4	1989	2	4
1936	1	5	1963	1	5	1990	1	5
1937	9	6	1964	9	6	1991	9	6
1938	8	7	1965	8	7	1992	8	7
1939	7	8	1966	7	8	1993	7	8
1940	6	9	1967	6	9	1994	6	9
1941	5	1	1968	5	1	1995	5	1
1942	4	2	1969	4	2	1996	4	2
1943	3	3	1970	3	3	1997	3	3
1944	2	4	1971	2	4	1998	2	4
1945	1	5	1972	1	5	1999	1	5
1946	9	6	1973	9	6	2000	9	6
1947	8	7	1974	8	7	2001	8	7
1948	7	8	1975	7	8	2002	7	8
1949	6	9	1976	6	9	2003	6	9
1950	5	1	1977	5	1	2004	5	1
1951	4	2	1978	4	2	2005	4	2
1952	3	3	1979	3	3	2006	3	3
1953	2	4	1980	2	4	2007	2	4
1954	1	5	1981	1	5	2008	1	5

YOUR PERSONALITY NUMBER

Use the following chart to calculate your Personality Number.
Identify your Basic Nature Number along the top then line it up with
your day/month down the side.

CHART OF YANG PERSONALITY NUMBERS

Basic Nature Number	1,4,7	2,5,8	3,6,9
Feb 4 – Mar 5	8	2	5
Mar 6 – April 4	7	1	4
April 5 – May 5	6	9	3
May 6 – June 5	5	8	2
June 6 – July 7	4	7	1
July 8 – Aug 7	3	6	9
Aug 8 – Sept 7	2	5	8
Sept 8 – Oct 8	1	4	7
Oct 9 – Nov 7	9	3	6
Nov 8 – Dec 7	8	2	5
Dec 8 – Jan 5	7	1	4
Jan 6 – Feb 3	6	9	3

A female born on March 12, 1962: Basic Nature Number 4, Personality Number 7
A male born on December 20, 1964: Basic Nature Number 9, Personality Number 4

Some of the more modern schools of Feng Shui use to this second number to ascertain
direction preferences, but most follow the traditional method used in this book.

The previous chart of Yang descending numbers is for males and females
up until the millennium as the present time represents a more materialistic,
Yang way of being. As we enter the twenty-first century – a more Yin period –
it is suggested that females may need to use their ascending Yin Personality
Number from the following chart.

CHART OF YIN PERSONALITY NUMBERS

Basic Nature Number	1,4,7	2,5,8	3,6,9
Feb 4 – Mar 5	7	4	1
Mar 6 – April 4	8	5	2
April 5 – May 5	9	6	3
May 6 – June 5	1	7	4
June 6 – July 7	2	8	5
July 8 – Aug 7	3	9	6
Aug 8 – Sept 7	4	1	7
Sept 8 – Oct 8	5	2	8
Oct 9 – Nov 7	6	3	9
Nov 8 – Dec 7	7	4	1
Dec 8 – Jan 5	8	5	2
Jan 6 – Feb 3	9	6	3

As humanity enters an age of greater spirituality, males may also find
their ascending Yin Personality Number becomes more appropriate.

THE ETERNALLY CHANGING EQUILIBRIUM OF YIN AND YANG

YOUR JOURNEY THROUGH

USE THE FOLLOWING CHART TO DETERMINE YOUR 3RD NUMBER – YOUR JOURNEY NUMBER.
In these sets of triple numbers, the 1st number is your Basic Nature Number,
the 2nd is your Personality Number, and the 3rd identifies your Journey Number.

The chart below reveals 108 character combinations.
If your Basic Number is 4 and your Personality Number is 9, your Journey Number will be 9: 4.9.9.
If your Basic Number is 8 and your Personality Number is 2, your Journey Number will be 2: 8.2.2.
If your Basic Number is 5 and your Personality Number is 7, your Journey Number will be 3: 5.7.3.

1.8.7	2.2.5	3.5.3	4.8.1	5.2.8	6.5.6	7.8.4	8.2.2	9.5.9
1.7.8	2.1.6	3.4.4	4.7.2	5.1.9	6.4.7	7.7.5	8.1.3	9.4.1
1.6.9	2.9.7	3.3.5	4.6.3	5.9.1	6.3.8	7.6.6	8.9.4	9.3.2
1.5.1	2.8.8	3.2.6	4.5.4	5.8.2	6.2.9	7.5.7	8.8.5	9.2.3
1.4.2	2.7.9	3.1.7	4.4.5	5.7.3	6.1.1	7.4.8	8.7.6	9.1.4
1.3.3	2.6.1	3.9.8	4.3.6	5.6.4	6.9.2	7.3.9	8.6.7	9.9.5
1.2.4	2.5.2	3.8.9	4.2.7	5.5.5	6.8.3	7.2.1	8.5.8	9.8.6
1.1.5	2.4.3	3.7.1	4.1.8	5.4.6	6.7.4	7.1.2	8.4.9	9.7.7
1.9.6	2.3.4	3.6.2	4.9.9	5.3.7	6.6.5	7.9.3	8.3.1	9.6.8
1.8.7	2.2.5	3.5.3	4.8.1	5.2.8	6.5.6	7.8.4	8.2.2	9.5.9
1.7.8	2.1.6	3.4.4	4.7.2	5.1.9	6.4.7	7.7.5	8.1.3	9.4.1
1.6.9	2.9.7	3.3.5	4.6.3	5.9.1	6.3.8	7.6.6	8.9.4	9.3.2

ARE YOU CURIOUS ABOUT

LIFE

風水

YOUR PATH IN LIFE ?
WHERE YOU WANT TO GO
... HOW AND WHY ?

YOUR 3RD NUMBER – JOURNEY NUMBER – INDICATES YOUR MOST SATISFYING PATH IN LIFE

IF YOUR JOURNEY NUMBER IS: WHATEVER YOUR PROFESSION, YOU FIND SATISFACTION IF YOU CAN:

1   Grow through your career: a career-based journey through life.

2   Become better integrated with parts of yourself and so understand others better – to live a life which creates peace, understanding, and harmony.

3   Be a loving authority (parent) to those in your area of influence and understand family dynamics and leadership – always generating anew.

4   Understand, appreciate, and create blessings in your life that are sometimes financial but not always. This is wealth in all its dimensions.

5   Unite – bring together – all the best parts of all the other eight numbers to live the bigger picture.

6   Serve by being a helpful friend to others – being an angel in other people's lives.

7   Tap into your creativity – invent – give birth to – set in motion a creative spark and foster its growth.

8   Deepen your knowledge of self and beyond – endeavor to live your life through conscious wisdom.

9   Live a life where your inner illumination inspires others – grow a reputation – be recognized.

ALTHOUGH THE STARS MAY INFLUENCE

OUR JOURNEY THROUGH LIFE –

THE CHOICES WE MAKE ON THAT JOURNEY ARE BASED ON

OUR PERSONAL HISTORY (PAST AND PRESENT) –

SO DESPITE IDENTICAL BIRTH DATES NO TWO INDIVIDUALS
WILL BE THE SAME

CHARACTER TYPES

THE CHARACTER TRAITS OF YOUR BASIC NATURE, PERSONALITY, AND JOURNEY NUMBERS ALL INFLUENCE HOW YOU INTERACT IN THE WORLD

1   Two sides: either gloomy, shy, and indecisive – or a passionate nature can surface as magnetic, vivacious, and charming. You're independent, talented, but better with strangers than with family. You are a good diplomat but have difficulty finishing things. You can appear shy and self-contained (out of balance, you are despondent).

2   Receptive, supportive, honest, and kind-hearted with a diplomatic nature. You have a natural need to tend to others but can sacrifice your own needs in the process. Considered a quiet person of action, you are generally reliable. You build experience slowly, and though you appear patient and pleasing, this may not always be natural (out of balance, you are critical).

3   Hasty, outgoing, and progressive. You are sensitive to criticism, are full of plans and enjoy initiating new projects. You do not like detail and your mind changes easily. You tend to take on too much and give the impression of chaos (out of balance, you are short-tempered).

4   Flexible, resilient, and gentle by nature you have penetrating insight – greatly appreciated by others. You have a tendency to become emotional and indecisive, and can be too trustworthy. You are easily influenced which can result in your being hurt … so get a second opinion. Strength comes from your flexibility – learn patience and trust your intuition (out of balance, you are short-tempered).

5   Strong, persistent, controlling, and sometimes domineering. Though sensitive to criticism, you are a survivor; there is a wildness to you and you work hard. You have an aptitude for leadership. Sometimes it is good to be in a situation where you risk failure in order to let go of your ego and deepen your self-knowledge (out of balance, you are skeptical).

6   You are magnanimous – straightforward, stylish – sincere and a perfectionist. You are sensitive to criticism and yet self-critical and defensive. Not comfortable in social situations, you can easily isolate yourself. You are down-to-earth and can manifest money easily. Since you are charming, careful, and organized you have great potential for leadership but can be uncompromising (out of balance, you are melancholy).

7   Flexible, sociable, entertaining, and soft on the inside. You can be hypersensitive, but you tend to hide your emotions. You can be a persuasive speaker with a naturally independent spirit. Your wit and charm helps others feel at ease. You can be passionate, changeable, and calculating. You need to use self-discipline to achieve success. You are very intuitive (out of balance, you are sad).

8   Naturally reserved though opinionated, you are self-motivated and persistent. Obstinate on the outside yet tender on the inside, you can be a little self-involved. You enjoy expression through music and the arts. Adventurous, energetic and introspective – 8 represents inner-knowledge (out of balance, you are irritable).

9   Flamboyant, sociable, proud, impulsive, and sometimes fickle. You are intelligent and very capable of leadership, but you must watch your vanity as this can make you too self-focused. You have a strong personality, are affectionate and honorable with a genuine interest in others. It is good if you can learn to play games and lose (out of balance, you are panicky and stressed).

MAN

男

女

WOMAN

COMBINED, THESE CHARACTERS READ

LOVE

COINCIDENCE?

Now that you know your three numbers

you can determine your compatibility

with others

PROFESSIONAL AND PERSONAL

和諧

COMPATIBILITY OR COMBATIBILITY

Your Basic Nature Number and Journey Number are the main influences in terms of compatibility, but if you are currently between 7 and 30 years old, your Personality Number is active during this time.

1 with 1:[1] They can be good together as long as they accept a balance. Being the same number they have an innate understanding of each other.

1 with 2: 2 tends to lean on number 1 – earth (2) clogs water (1).

1 with 3: 1 (water) is manipulative in business – 3 (wood) is intuitive – this is a good combination.

1 with 4: The seriousness of 1 (water) combines well with the gentle wisdom of 4 (wood).

1 with 5: Earth (5) clogs water (1), creating confusion.[2]

1 with 6: 1 (water) is a good communicator and 6 (metal) is straightforward – good combination. Metal supports water.

1 with 7: Both are good communicators – metal (7) supports water (1).

1 with 8: Can be exhausting – they are so different – earth (8) clogs water (1).

1 with 9: Careful 1 (water) can put out the expressive, impulsive fire of 9.

2 with 2: They tend to criticize each other – patience is the key.

2 with 3: Quick 3 (wood) needs to be patient with slower 2 (earth).

2 with 4: Not an easy combination – 2 (earth) is conservative – 4 (wood) is dynamic.

2 with 5: This is good as long as 2 (earth) follows 5 (earth).

2 with 6: This is good as long as 2 (earth) follows 6 (metal).

2 with 7: This is good as long as 2 (earth) follows 7 (metal).

2 with 8: 2 (earth) is very nurturing – so 8 (earth) feels safe here. Being opposite corners of the Lo Shu grid, they help bring balance to each other.

2 with 9: This is a good relationship – expressive 9 (fire) supports nurturing 2 (earth).

3 with 3: This can be good but they need to be patient with each other.

3 with 4: This can be a good combination if they make an effort to understand each other.

3 with 5: This could be a power struggle – they are a bit too direct for each other.

3 with 6: This is good if 6 (metal) can learn to tolerate 3 (wood).

3 with 7: Care needs to be taken here.

3 with 8: 3 (wood) is open – 8 (earth) is reserved – a difficult combination.

3 with 9: A very good combination.

BETWEEN THE DIFFERENT NUMBERS

4 with 4: A good combination even though they stand slightly apart from each other.

4 with 5: Not easy, 5 (earth) attempts to dominate 4's (wood) gentleness.

4 with 6: Can be good (being opposite corners of the Lo Shu grid helps them overcome their differences); 4 (wood) is emotional – 6 (metal) is straightforward.

4 with 7: They get along because they are both flexible.

4 with 8: Not an easy combination – 8 (earth) is self-involved – 4 (wood) is too trusting.

4 with 9: This combination is good. Insightful 4 (wood) feeds gregarious 9 (fire).

5 with 5: Their strong controlling natures create conflict.

5 with 6: There is mutual respect here – earth (5) creates metal (6).

5 with 7: There is mutual respect here for 5's strength (earth) and 7's elegance (metal).

5 with 8: This is a good combination as 5 (earth) gains admiration for 8's (earth) persistence.

5 with 9: Opposites attract – 9's refinement (fire) enjoys 5's wildness (earth) and vice versa.

6 with 6: Can be good if they can learn to be magnanimous with each other.

6 with 7: They must be careful with each other – 7 (little metal) is more sensitive than 6 (strong metal).

6 with 8: This is good and even better if 8 (earth) lets 6 (metal) lead.

6 with 9: Not a good combination – 9's flamboyance (fire) clashes with 6's down-to-earth manner (metal).

7 with 7: It's difficult for real friendship to grow as they both hide their feelings.

7 with 8: They respect each other.

7 with 9: They are uncomfortable with each other – 9 (fire) can melt 7 (little metal).

8 with 8: Their obstinate and self-motivated habits get in the way of a good relationship.

8 with 9: 9 (fire) admires 8's (earth) persistence – 8 admires 9's leadership qualities.

9 with 9: This combination could be good if they can see the bigger picture and not let vanity get in the way.

1 These numbers are also represented by elements on the star cycle, see page 148.
2 Compensating for incompatibility is explained on page 149.

HOW YOUR ELEMENT AND CHINESE ANIMAL IMPACT ON YOUR CHARACTER

THE INTERACTION OF YOUR ELEMENT, ANIMAL, AND CHARACTER TYPE NUMBERS WILL OBVIOUSLY RESULT IN MODIFICATION OF YOUR CHARACTER TRAITS AND RESULTING COMPATIBILITY.

THIS IS PART OF WHAT GIVES HUMANITY ITS RICH TAPESTRY AND SURPRISE.

ELEMENT CHARACTERISTICS

WATER   Persuasive – diplomatic – tends to be deep and reflective.

EARTH   Sensitive – practical and dependable – down-to-earth (literally) – nurturing of others – can be stubborn.

WOOD   Energetic – self-confident – ethical – born leader – progressive – benevolent – not very good at completing tasks.

METAL   Righteous – independent – ambitious – determined – inflexible – natural authority.

FIRE   Charismatic – creative – decisive – clever – generous – passionate – ambitious – sociable.

The element of your year of birth may be different to the element of your character numbers (see page 155).

CHINESE ANIMALS

In Chinese astrology, time is divided into sixty-year cycles. These are made up of the twelve years (twelve Chinese animal signs) and the five elements – 12 x 5 = 60 ... so every sixty years there will be a metal rat, every sixty years a fire ox, etc.

ANIMAL CHARACTERISTICS (see chart on page 55)

RAT   Social – innovative – ambitious – secretive

OX   Methodical – materialistic – reliable – charitable

TIGER   Sincere – a survivor – romantic – reckless

RABBIT   Peaceful – humorous – sensible – elegant manner

DRAGON   Loyal – courageous – great integrity – tending to arrogance

SNAKE   Profound thinker – wise – intuitive powers – gentle cunning – charismatic

HORSE   Quick-witted – friendly – popular – often successful but can be fickle

SHEEP   Romantic – honorable – generous – can be a bit negative

MONKEY   Playful – quick-witted – adaptable – inventive

ROOSTER   Proud – efficient – can be critical

DOG   Reliable – cynical – loyal – displays cool independence but can be warm

PIG   Kind-hearted – resilient – amenable – can be superficial

THE FOLLOWING ANIMAL SIGNS ARE COMPATIBLE WITH EACH OTHER:

RAT – DRAGON – MONKEY[1]   Impatient, loyal, desire success
OX – SNAKE – ROOSTER   Intellectual, loyal
TIGER – HORSE – DOG   Great camaraderie between them
RABBIT – SHEEP – PIG   Compassionate

THE FOLLOWING ANIMAL SIGNS ARE THE LEAST COMPATIBLE WITH EACH OTHER:[2]

RAT – HORSE
OX – SHEEP
MONKEY – TIGER
DOG – DRAGON
RABBIT – ROOSTER
SNAKE – PIG

Despite the fact that the same animal signs understanding each other, which can aid compatibility, they may have a tendency to criticize each other since they are so alike.

Each person has good and bad years relative to their personal animal sign and its compatibility with the animal sign of a particular year. For example, if you are a tiger, you would have had a difficult year in the year of the monkey, 1992, but would have had a good year in 1990, the year of the horse.

A difficult year could be a sensitive time for you, so be aware of this when you attend to the Feng Shui in your home and office during that period and don't overstimulate the environment (see page 151).

1 Each Chinese animal has an equivalent zodiac sign for Western astrology, see page 155.
2 More information about compatibility is given on page 148.

YOU CAN CHANGE YOUR LIFE

IF YOU ARE WILLING TO CHANGE YOUR THINKING

選擇

REMEMBER:

YOU ALWAYS HAVE A CHOICE

When Einstein came up with the particle and wave theory, he kept his discovery quiet for years because he feared the establishment would think he was crazy.

Many intangible concepts are greeted with skepticism.

Allow the possibility with Feng Shui.
You just might find it worth the effort.

"WE SHALL NOT CEASE FROM EXPLORATION
AND THE END OF OUR EXPLORING
WILL BE TO ARRIVE WHERE WE STARTED
AND KNOW THE PLACE
FOR THE FIRST TIME."

T.S. Eliot (Four Quartets)

吸入

INHALE

■

發散

EXHALE

■

THE BREATH

呼吸

LIFE FORCE

CHI

WE ARE MORE THAN THE SUM OF OUR PARTS

氣

風水

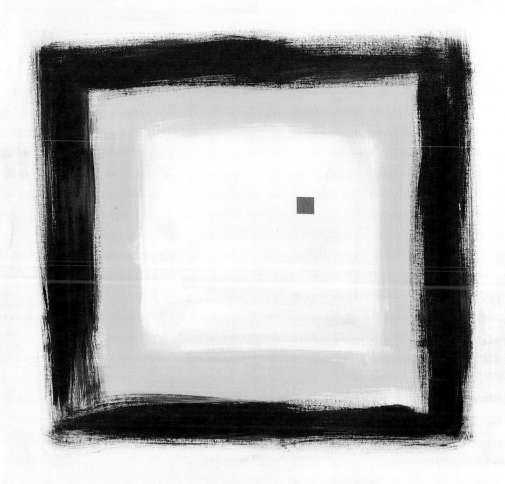

SO IS OUR ENVIRONMENT

HERE ARE OVER 400 SUGGESTIONS

ROOM BY ROOM

SITUATION BY SITUATION

ON HOW TO APPLY FENG SHUI

RECOMMENDATIONS FOR
THE OFFICE AND WORK AREA

IN A BUILDING, IT IS IMPORTANT TO
CONSCIOUSLY CONSIDER SPACE, PROPORTION,
LIGHTING, FURNITURE, COLOR, THE ELEMENTS,
AND THE SURROUNDING LANDSCAPE.

風水

If you wish to have a more in-depth understanding of the
theory of Feng Shui, turn to page 147 before reading these
suggestions.

Business Feng Shui is affected by many merging forces
that need to be kept in balance to create harmony. This
concept of balance extends beyond environmental design
to the business's sign board, its logo, even the business
cards of its representatives.

For logos, use colors and shapes that are compatible with
the element of your Kua Number (see page 54) or that of
the nature of your business. Avoid triangles with the point
at the bottom – it represents a filter with your wealth
pouring away.

Check the image of the office and the first impression you
get when you walk through the door. This has a subtle
effect on you and your visitors' attitude. If a company
looks good when a client walks in, they will have more
confidence in you. Be aware that the images and pictures
you have on the walls impact visitors and set the mood for
the office. Are the colors and images inspiring – do they
reflect the culture of the company?

When choosing art for the wall, make sure you like it. Do
not put up an image because others like it. Remember
image is symbolic. If you put up an image of conflict or
battle in your relationship corner, you are likely to
introduce combat into your relationship. The best kind of
image to put in the relationship corner is one of harmony
and union.

The main door of your home or office should face at least one of your good directions (see page 56).

Is it easy to recognize which is the doorway into the main office when a client arrives?

If you have one direction of energy coming in through the main lobby to a building and another direction coming into your office, it is the one coming into your office that has the priority power.

If you share a hallway with another tenant in your home or office, your boundary on the grid is your own door and does not include the hallway. If this communal hallway creates negative space (see negative space, page 152) place some of your personal pictures or plants in it so that you energetically reclaim it.

Make sure that the foyer is well lit and that all bulbs are working.

Thresholds and doormats should not bear your company's logo as this represents people walking all over you.

Generally it is the chief executive's location that has the greatest impact on the success of a business, so it is preferable not to locate it at the end of a long corridor.

If possible, do not sit in the section of the office that represents a nonsupportive location for you.

Where there is an L-shaped room and a mirror can't be used to create the illusion of a square, set up a visual barrier using furniture or a book shelf, e.g., or change a section of the floor covering to create the impression of two rectangles (see mirrors on page 126).

Position furniture to give you the broadest view of the room and doorway.[1]

1 For specific information for desk positions, see pages 104-7

If there are two people in a room, one with their back to the window and one with their back to the wall, the one with their back to the wall will be in a more powerful position.

Do not place refuse bins in the Southeast (wealth) corner and, wherever you put them, empty them often.

Place inspiring images straight ahead of you – these raise your personal Chi.

Have the windows facing you or to the side of you.

If there is a structural beam above your head in your office, hang a mobile or wind chime from it to interrupt the suppressing energy – or avoid sitting under it altogether. In China, they place two bamboo flutes hung by a red ribbon at 45 degrees to each other to raise the Chi.

Places that are over-furnished will make you feel wedged in or stuck, so clear the space of unnecessary clutter.

If you have low ceilings, hang pictures of birds or other images of rising energy (sunrise) or place uplighters (lights where the direction of illumination is upwards) under the low section.

Water represents money, so images of water pouring in – such as a waterfall – are very auspicious in the Southeast. The element of the Southeast is wood, so the image of a flourishing tree would be good, too.

If your windows do not open, and you have several computers and copiers which are generating electromagnetic charges – introduce some plants. These absorb the negative Chi while simultaneously emanating positive Chi (see plants, page 128).

Allow as much sunlight and fresh air as possible to enter your environment – this enhances Chi.

Avoid an office that directly faces an escalator or elevator as these take energy away.

Hong Kong Shanghai Bank – Foster & Partners

Feng Shui experts were brought in throughout the project and the Hong Kong Shanghai Bank even went to the expense of purchasing the land in front of its site and donated it to the Government to guarantee that they would have open space – park and view – in front of their building where positive Chi could accumulate. The hills behind the city act as protection.

If there is a window directly facing you when you open the door, the Chi will simply come in and go out again. Set up some kind of screen with plants or bookshelves, for example, so that the energy will first have to meander and travel further into the room.

Too many doors and windows disperse Chi. Treat the windows with blinds or curtains to help contain the Chi and keep closed any doors that are not needed. Windows should open outwards.

In instances of unusual buildings, such as an elongated L-shape or a Y-shaped building, consider each wing as independent of the other and place a number of grids accordingly.

Draw the layout of the office – then run a line from the door around the furniture – how smooth or congested is the flow? Always place your furniture to create ease of movement.

Check out the Basic Nature Number of partners, associates, and people you are going to work with – if there is more than one, try to align yourself with the number that is most compatible with yours (see page 78).

If there is a cash register located in the Southeast (wealth area), reflect it in a mirror to double your money.

Make sure there is no cutting Chi directed at the cash register (see page 136).

If there are images that in any way deplete your inspiration or have negative associations – remove them.

Camouflage toilet doors in an office while still indicating somehow its location.

If you believe the problems you are having are creating blocks – heaviness – frustration, apply a symbol that is open, light, and that suggests ease of movement.

If your office is aligned to one of your preferred directions or locations, Feng Shui is generally well taken care of, but it is seldom practical for everyone in an office to get everything perfect, so often one must make compromises. If the space that you are in is not one of your most supportive areas of the building, nor one of your most supportive directions, or if perhaps you even have to work with your back to the door – apply one of the colors and elements to compensate and support you (see pages 150 and 154).

It is undesirable to have your office or home at the end of a cul-de-sac or a no-exit street. These allow possible stagnation of energy and the buildings can lack inspiration.

Trees at the back of your building represent protection.

Staircase design should preferably be curving and wide – spirals are to be avoided (like a corkscrew boring a hole). If this is not possible, place plants under the spiral.

To prevent energy from racing down the steps on a staircase, put a bright image on the wall at the top of the stairs. Stairs are better if they have risers at the back instead of open treads – if not, put plants or illumination behind them. You are less likely to trip due to spatial distraction.

If a staircase runs down to your main door, place a reflective object on the inside of the door to reflect the energy back into your office (on the front door of your home too) – this is especially important if a staircase then also descends from outside your door.

You do not want stairs to be too steep or too narrow.

In the Orient, the number of steps is considered to be very important – the recommended numbers are: 1 – 2 – 5 – 10 – 13 – 14 – 17 – 22 – 25 – 26 – etc. (i.e. no whole multiples of 3 or 4). The origin of this is unclear.

Centuries ago Plato and Pythagoras made references to the power of numbers and proportion in building design

If something in your life seems to be stuck, check where you have some heavy immovable object – and MOVE IT. If window panes, mirrors, or lights are broken, fix them.

Background music that is appropriate to the work can be nurturing and inspiring. Beautiful music is soothing to the soul as it affects our mood, so be sure to choose the music with care.

If there is a lamp post or a tree directly outside your door, balance this vertical blockage by putting some ceramic pots on either side of your doorway.

In the Orient it is common to find eight coins tied together with a red ribbon hung on the wall in the Northwest or Southeast. This is believed to attract good luck and prosperity.

Offices with good Feng Shui rarely have problems with absenteeism.

AIM FOR SIMPLICITY – THINK CREATIVELY.

TRUST YOUR INTUITION.

THE STUDY

Fresh flowers on the desk stimulate energy – and encourage clearer thinking.

A quartz crystal on a desk also encourages clarity – keep it a distance from the computer, though, as it absorbs and radiates the electromagnetic energy.

Place a bright reading lamp on the desk, preferably in the South (fame, reputation) to inspire a bright future.

The Pyramid at the Louvre – I.M. Pei

Pyramid shapes are associated with tombs – so this building is considered very Yin. Its shape and material is like an enormous crystal bringing Yang sunlight into its Yin interior.

THE CHARACTERISTICS OF YOUR JOURNEY NUMBER IN THE WORKPLACE

IF YOUR
JOURNEY NUMBER IS

1 You are independent and paternal.

2 You are conservative and dependent – a little touchy but very patient.

3 You are sharp, active, and sensitive. This sensitivity comes from the heart so you tend to be very self-protective.

4 You are active, evasive, impatient, and emotional – with a tender expression, it is important that you explain clearly what you mean.

5 You can be a very potent force.

6 You have a strong will and tend to want to control things – your clarity is respected.

7 You are flexible and sensitive – you desire financial success.

8 You are highly self-motivated with lots of energy – but you have a tendency to avoid responsibility.

9 You are always seeking recognition – you are a good talker with a tendency to exaggerate. You are passionate but lack patience.

OUR CONTEMPORARY UNDERSTANDING

OF THE PSYCHOLOGY OF DESIGN,

COLOR THEORY AND ERGONOMICS ARE INHERENT

TO THE PRINCIPLES OF FENG SHUI,

SO IT IS A GREAT DESIGN TOOL.

風水

THE WONDERFUL PARADOX OF FENG SHUI IS

THAT SOMETHING SO ANCIENT

CAN BE SO CUTTING EDGE

保護

THE PREDECESSOR LAW

One of the most important principles to understand in Feng Shui is the Predecessor Law – the vibration that remains in the environment from those who lived or worked there before you.

You may have heard about the experience of someone moving into a new house and getting divorced soon afterwards – later they discover that many of the people who had moved in before them had also separated. It may be that the relationship sector of the building is at fault and that the energy vibration of disharmony is being magnified each time people move in and split.

If the previous tenants of your office had financial troubles ending in bankruptcy, then the environment still carries that energy. This can make it more difficult for your business to succeed. Cleansing the building (see page 134) and enhancing it can transform this blockage – apply Feng Shui principles and change the luck.

If the prior tenants enjoyed great success, the chances are that that energy will help you towards greater success.

DESK AREA

At work, the location of your office or desk is extremely important to harness good Chi and benefit your career or business – and so enhance your life.

Get your desk and work area in order – it is a reflection of your mental state and vice versa.

Be sure to face one of your preferred directions.

On your desk put a small arrow indicating your preferred direction (see page 56). If you wish, you can also place an arrow for your second direction. This will remind you to adopt your best direction – a quick glance at your arrow and you can align yourself to your power position.

If you sit facing one of your supportive directions you will feel more clearer headed and calm.

If your best direction has cutting Chi directed at it that you cannot avoid, apply your second or third direction (see page 56). Do not place yourself in your best direction regardless.

When you are sitting at your desk, make sure that you can see who is entering your workspace. If your back is to the entrance, it can create unease which energetically will tire you sooner.

If you cannot see the door and you can't move your desk, strategically place a mirror so you can see the door. At home this is not as vital as it is a more protected environment.

Preferably, there should be no passageway behind a desk – so you cannot be surprised from behind.

Do not sit with your back to the window – this suggests a lack of support – a solid wall behind you is best.

First determine the placement of your desk, then arrange the bookcase and the filing cabinets and any other furniture you may have.

There should be easy access to your desk. Remove obstacles!

It is best to have the desk facing into a room rather than facing a wall. If you do have to place the desk against a wall and you are right-handed, have the window on your left (or the right for left-handed people).

Square or rectangular desks are good for commercial enterprises and hard-line negotiating.

Curved, oval, or round desks are best for environments where creativity is a first priority, but too many curves and you may not manage your money well.

Curved desks are good in a reception area – try to keep electrical and telephone wires out of sight or tidy.

A reflective desk surface distracts, creating fatigue sooner.

Black desks can diminish productivity as black absorbs energy.

If your drawing board is white you may work more slowly, so put a contrast around the edge.

Have direct lighting over the desk if possible.

Do not sit under high shelving units or you will feel that "everything is getting on top of you."

Check what is in your relationship corner – the Southwest. If you do not have a relationship but would like one, place an image that symbolizes togetherness and place pairs of things in that area.

Place your telephone in the Northwest corner – helpful friends.

The Northeast (knowledge corner) is a good location to keep reference information.

If your money seems to vanish before your eyes, you need to weigh down your wealth area (the Southeast). Put something solid there – possibly a heavy sculpture – and give that corner some extra light.

To boost your creativity, put something directly in front of you on your desk that links to your dreams – a picture – a book cover – something that inspires you.

Strong artwork on the wall behind your desk will distract visitors during their discussions with you.

The size and proportion of doors and windows are important. According to contemporary Feng Shui, the following dimensions are recommended for desks (though the source of this information is unclear). If your desk does not comply with the above but feels good – keep it – instincts are part of the essence of Feng Shui.

Measurements for desks: the length should be 106.5–112 cm (42– 44 in), 124.5–132 cm (49–52 in), or 145–155 cm (57–61 in) – the depth and height should be 84 cm (33 in).

Any multiple of 43 cm (17 in), added to the above is indicative of a good room size (though the origin of this statistic is similarly unclear). Let your instincts decide for you.

Single desks are preferable to U-shaped arrangements, which can cause friction. Desks placed face to face are considered confrontational.

Make sure you have a chair that supports your spine and is comfortable.

Fatigue in the office environment often comes from excess positive ions in the air created by the electronic machinery and lack of oxygen. One way to increase negative ions in the air is to wash the surface of your desk daily with water – or use an ionizer.

EXAMPLES TO HELP YOU IN YOUR OFFICE

OFFICE 1

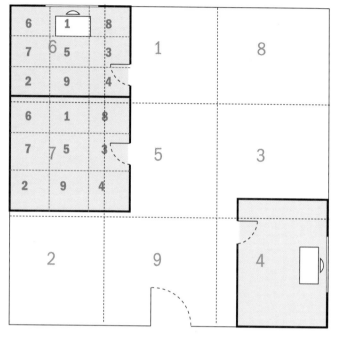

ENTRANCE TO MAIN OFFICE

OFFICE 2

In this office, the occupant's birthday is May 28, 1965. So his Kua Number is 8 and he belongs to the West group.

Sitting in the North location of his individual office is not supportive (see Preferred Directions chart, page 56).

Facing South direction is not supportive.

With the window behind him, he is sitting in his own shadow, creating vulnerability.

In terms of the whole main office grid, he is sitting in location 6 (Northwest). This location is good for him although he could reposition himself to be sitting in location 2 (Southwest) diagonally facing 8 (Northeast). By facing Northeast, the energy supports him.

6	1	8
7	5	3
2	9	4

The above becomes a grid for the desk also.
Enhance the location and direction of this desk in the manner suggested throughout this book.

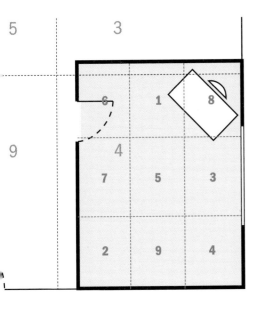

OFFICE 2: EXAMPLE LAYOUT A

In this office, the occupant's date of birth is May 19, 1962, so his Kua Number is 2 and again he would belong to the West group.

So the Northeast location (8) supports him.

His back is to a solid wall.

He can see the door.

West (7) energy coming through the door supports him and he is facing Southwest (2) – all of which are his supportive directions.

The desk position in Layout A (left) is good for him, but the desk position in Layout B (below) is not good for him.

In terms of the whole office, he is sitting in location 4 (Southeast). This location is not one of his best so he should bring in the elements and colors that support him: earth and fire (see pages 150 and 151).

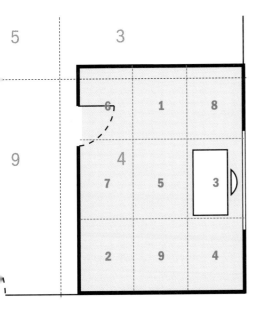

OFFICE 2: EXAMPLE LAYOUT B

Here in Layout B, however, the occupant's birthday is September 10, 1953. Her Kua Number is 4 and she belongs to the East group.

She is sitting in the East location (3), which is supportive for her.

She can also see the door, which is good.

Unfortunately, she has her back to a window, so she will feel vulnerable.

Energy coming into the room is West (7) energy, which does not support her, but the energy coming into the main office is coming from the South (9), which compensates.

In terms of the whole main office, she is sitting in location 4 (Southeast), which is good for her.

BUSINESS LOCATIONS

Place your personnel managers and human resources in the East (representing harmony and cooperation).

Put your research people and human resources in the Northeast – this governs knowledge.

The chief financial advisors of the company, as well as stockbrokers and traders, should sit in the Southeast (representing wealth). Use black and navy in the decor and the logo. Place profits, accounts, and the office cash register in the Southeast.

Secretaries should sit in the Northwest (representing helpful friends).

If the office is engaged in entertainment or magazine media, then the important members of the company should sit in the South or Southeast sectors (representing fame and wealth).

If your business is dealing with finance, bank investment, or insurance – then your element is water – incorporate navy and black (colors for water) and place young trainees and new staff in the North (represents water) or West (supports water). (See star cycle, page 149).

Property developers, architects, and real estate people should be in the Southwest, or put them in the Southeast and apply Southwest colors. Stimulate earth sectors of the office (see page 151).

Farming, gardening, and furniture manufacturing are represented by the wood element, so these enterprises should activate their East (3) and Southeast (4) sectors.

Companies that work with metal (such as steel, jewelry) should activate their Northwest and West sectors – avoid red, though, as it melts metal (see page 148).

DOORS

Your front door is considered your main door. If, in your household, everyone uses the back door, then this should be considered your main door and it is the energy coming in through this door that you need to assess. Entrance doors should enter inwards, drawing in the Chi.

The design and location of doors is important for the quality of the flow of Chi into the room or building. In the Far East, if the door does not face a supportive direction, they use or create another door.

It is better to have a back door so the Chi can circulate in and out and not stagnate. If this is not possible, keep a window opposite the door slightly ajar.

The door should open to the fullness of the room rather than opening to a wall. If this is not possible, then place a mirror on the adjacent wall that you open on to – this expands the Chi.

Chi enters through your front door, so make sure your entrance is welcoming, preferably opening into a spacious and well-lit interior.

Have a strong and solid main door representing strength and stability.

Doors that directly face each other in a corridor can cause conflict – use subtle colors and soft lighting to neutralize this situation. Ideally, doors should be opposite solid walls.

In a corridor, if doors partially face each other, place a mirror to deflect the energy from the opposite door.

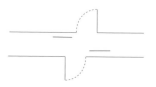

Where doors are congested and could knock into each other, replace with a sliding door or curtain.

A blocked door symbolizes something blocked in your life. Should you plan to close off a door completely, be sure to put some sea salt inside the cavity – this will absorb any trapped and stagnant Chi.

The front door should preferably not face the edge of an elevated freeway – there is too much racing Chi and you will feel unsettled.

Doors that are too large or too small in proportion to the overall size of the room are strongly discouraged.

The entrance to a shop needs to be carefully designed to attract customers. It should not be so small that it impedes entry or too large as to allow Chi to flow right out again. Revolving doors are very good.

If you are choosing a color for the door, see the chart on page 124.

Doors facing churches or monasteries can have imbalance because of the massive Yin energy being exerted – paint the door one of the Yang colors, such as red (see page 122).

FENG SHUI IS NO MAGIC WAND

BUT IT CAN BRING HARMONY
TO AN ENVIRONMENT

IF YOUR ENVIRONMENT IS BALANCED WHEN
YOU ARE COMMUNICATING WITH PEOPLE,
YOU WILL DO SO WITH MORE EASE.

WITH THE RESULT THAT
AN OPPORTUNITY MAY COME YOUR WAY.

THAT OPPORTUNITY MAY CHANGE YOUR LIFE.

RECOMMENDATIONS FOR THE HOME

家

WORKING TOWARD DOMESTIC BLISS

FENG SHUI REQUIRES AN INTEGRATED APPROACH. IF YOU COME INTO THE OFFICE HAVING SLEPT WELL AND FEELING GOOD, THE RESULTS WILL SHOW IN YOUR WORK. APPLY THESE PRINCIPLES IN YOUR HOME – ESPECIALLY IN YOUR BEDROOM – YOU SPEND ABOUT ONE-THIRD OF YOUR LIFE THERE.

Check the direction of the main front door and that of the master bedroom.

Ensure that sunlight comes into the building – preferably in the main living areas.

The element of the head of the household should be represented in all the main living areas. In the individual bedrooms, it should be the element of their occupant.

THE MAIN BEDROOM

The balance in this room affects the whole household.

Check the direction and location of this room and the bed.

If a husband and wife are in different number groups, then the front door alignment should support him and the bed alignment should support her or vice versa (see page 57).

Activate the corner that relates to career success – place a bright light there.

You want a broad view of the room from your bed and to be able to see the door.

Do not sleep under a structural beam – if you do and it spans across the middle, it can cause discomfort and possible illness – if it divides you and your partner it can encourage separation – beams disturb sleep. If you can't avoid it – create a canopy over the bed to act as a shield (see page 96).

Always have a solid wall behind the bed – not a window.

It is preferable to avoid sleeping with your head to a wall that backs on to a toilet. If there is no choice, affix reflective foil on the back of your bedhead. It is also preferable to have a bedhead that is solid.

When you are lying in bed avoid having your feet point to the door. If you have no choice, put some kind of barrier there such as a cabinet. The reason is that mythically you are carried out feet first when you die.

If you are forced to choose between two poor alternatives, it is more important that your head aligns with your best direction, than that your feet do not point toward the door.

It is preferable not to have your head towards the door wall as you are instinctively on alert for unseen dangers – tribal response, like our ancestor, the caveman. If there is no choice, position a mirror so that you can see the door from the bed but not so that it reflects you as you sleep (see page 126).

The bedroom is especially appropriate for relationship enhancements, so pay special attention to the Southwest corner (place romantic images here – images of union, pairs of things). Mineral crystals are good here – representing earth element. Two rose quartz crystals placed in the Southwest would enhance a loving relationship.

Check the direction that you are facing at your dressing table when getting ready for work each morning – harness one of your supportive directions.

If the relationship section – the Southwest – is missing in your home or bedroom (negative space, see page 152) place a mirror to transcend this absent space (see mirrors on page 126).

Avoid installing your toilet in the Southwest sector – if it is already there and you have a second toilet, use that instead.

Clear clutter from under the bed as this can create negative Chi which may be absorbed during sleep. Even if things are neatly stored under the bed – move them or somehow allow an air gap.

Let the image facing you as you wake up be uplifting. Start the day well, the first image you see has a deep unconscious impact.

It is preferable for the bedroom door not to be too close to the entrance of your home or you will become more focused on resting.

Have things around you that you love – if anything has a negative association, put it away or give it away. It will tend to deplete your energy whenever you look at it (perhaps a gift from someone you do not like or something that has a sad memory).

Have round edges on your night tables – or cover any sharp edges with a cloth to prevent cutting Chi being directed towards you while you sleep (see page 136).

Avoid water paintings and aquariums in the main bedroom, as union is represented by the earth element and water makes this soggy.

No fresh flowers in the bedroom, these are energizing and so do not aid sleep.

Use a hot water bottle rather than an electric blanket.

If something is broken – fix it.

CHILDREN'S ROOMS

The West location is good as this represents joy, creativity, and resting energy (sunset). The East represents rising energy – if you require more invigorating energy for the child in that room.

The Southwest is a good location for a daughter – it encourages a good relationship for her later in life.

The 4th direction is good for the bed (the direction of energy coming in through the crown of their head – spirit energy) (see page 56).

No aggressive images in this room – they have a subconscious effect.

Place family pictures on the walls in the East (family roots).

Place images of their own creativity on the West wall.

Use colors appropriate to the child's number (see page 150).

Use gentle tones – bright colors can be overstimulating.

In the South (reputation) place images and documents relating to their aspirations.

A mobile hung over a baby's head is stimulating and not restful, so place it near the foot of the cot where the baby can focus on it comfortably from a distance.

THE DINING ROOM

The ideal location for the dining room is in the center of the building.

Yellows or soft peaches are good in this room as they unite, gather, and invigorate.

Do not place tall decorations on the table as these can create a communication block during dinner.

If you have a glass-top table, cover it with a tablecloth when entertaining as the reflection and transparency can be distracting or tiring. Your guests may leave early.

Round tables represent heaven's blessings.

Mirrors are very good in the dining room as they double the nourishment (inner nourishment).

Chairs need to be comfortable and supportive.

Focusing on time can cause indigestion, so no clocks here.

Candles are good at a gathering, creating vibrant energy.

Place shy guest in the position from where they can see the door – they will tend to feel more confident.

Paintings of food or of people enjoying themselves are good on the walls here.

THE KITCHEN AND BATHROOM

The kitchen is considered one of the more important rooms because it is where the food is prepared and food represents inner wealth and well-being.

If the first thing you see on entering the environment is the kitchen door, you may start eating more. Similarly, you do not want to see the bathroom immediately as this flushes away wealth. So set up some kind of screen or place a mirror on the bathroom door so that it is concealed in a decorative way.

Although kitchens and ovens are not to be located in your most auspicious locations, it is beneficial if your oven harnesses one of your preferred directions (see page 56).

It is better if kitchens and bathrooms are delegated to areas that are considered less supportive (5th to 8th locations).

Fire and water should not be placed next to each other – placing ovens next to sinks or refrigerators can cause conflicts. A wooden chopping board or small plant on the counter mitigates the conflict of fire with water – a photograph or painting of plants will do. (See the mitigating cycle on page 148.)

Do not place the oven under a window as this encourages the energy to leave.

It is preferable if the front of your oven does not face the main door – to prevent good Chi from leaving.

Make toilet areas small and inconspicuous.

Once you have identified the wealth or career section of your building, guard against locating your toilets in these sections if at all possible. If this is not possible, display an image which represents the element of the Southeast (4) such as pictures of plants on its walls.

Check the toilets and sinks are in good working order. If they leak, it is wasteful and a sign of leaking finances. Attend to any blockages and keep plugs in bath and sink wastes.

Keep bathroom doors closed.

In the bathroom, keep the lid down on the toilet as this is considered to be an open channel to the sewers of your city.

Put sea salt in small containers in bathroom areas as this absorbs negative Chi. (Replace weekly.)

Place a small convex mirror or something reflective on the outside of the door to deflect good energy from going down the toilet.

Your least auspicious locations are best for the kitchen, toilet, or storeroom. It is considered that in this way the less supportive luck is "pressed down."

THE GARDEN

Place the grid onto your garden plot and use the principles of color and symbol.

Feng Shui is based on the principle of the balancing of opposites Yin and Yang.

Zigzag patterns reflect mountains – Yang. Meandering paths represent water – Yin.

Rock gardens in a pond represent harmony – the rocks are symbols of mountains – Yang – and the water is Yin – perfect balance.

Create curving paths in your garden rather than straight ones.

Large leafed plants are Yang … delicate leaves like ferns are Yin.
Tall trees are Yang … horizontal foliage is Yin.
Light is Yang … shade is Yin.
Red flowers are Yang … violet flowers are Yin.

White orchids represent femininity and endurance.
Yellow roses represent intellect – red roses, beauty.
Tulips represent love – chrysanthemums, happiness.
Geraniums represent abundance.
Jasmine represents communication and friendship and is Yin.
Peonies represent wealth and honor and are Yang.
Bamboo represents growth and is Yang.
Willow represents grace and is Yin.

In the garden, enhance areas in specific ways:

In the West – place a metal wind chime and flowers whose colors are blue, white, or yellow. Round shapes are good here.

In the Northwest – put a stone sculpture – yellow and orange flowers – round shapes here.

In the Southwest – this is a good place for a bird bath – yellow, orange, and red flowers – square shapes here.

In the North – a good place for a water feature – blue flowers – wavy shapes here.

In the Northeast – place a rock garden with red and yellow flowering plants – square shapes here.

In the East – a proliferation of green – plant tall trees – rectangular shapes here.

In the Southeast – a small waterfall represents money pouring in – a pond represents success – plant leafy plants and trees such as willows – rectangular shapes here.

In the South – plant triangular fir trees or pine trees and red flowers – triangular shapes here. Study the shapes and apply the star cycle principles on page 150.

Pine, willow, and cypress trees are especially auspicious.

Evergreen hedges are preferred as these suggest longevity.

An eight-sided pagoda represents prosperity; five-sided represents the elements.

Place wooden furniture in the East and Southeast (or South) and metal furniture in the Northwest and West (and North). See the star cycle on page 148.

If you have sculptures in the garden, make sure their image is friendly rather than aggressive (similarly inside a building, although an aggressive sculpture such as a roaring lion could be used externally as a defensive tactic).

The equivalent to clutter in a garden is a neglected, overgrown one. Your outer world reflects your inner world – so taking care of your garden is like taking care of yourself.

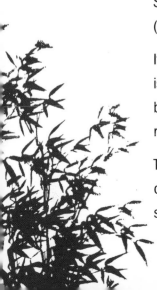

COLOR

Color can raise or lower our spirits – increase or deplete our energy – creating a sense of concentration or distraction. Ignore what interior design dictates unless it feels good to YOU.

White, which represents metal, is the color of innocence and is the source of all colors. Too much can distract, so hang lots of images on the walls to spread the energy. White is good in the Southwest, Northwest, and North.

Gray is cooling and represents metal. It is good in the West and Northwest.

Black, which represents water and money, is powerful and absorbs other colors. If used excessively it can create a depressing environment, diminishing your physical energy.

Red (fire element), although representing happiness to the Chinese, must be used with care – it is a most auspicious color and the most highly charged wavelength in the visual spectrum and although it can attract dynamic creativity, too much can create conflict.

Bedrooms are Yin – places of rest – so avoid red. It could cause insomnia.

Also avoid red in children's rooms as it can create hyperactivity. (Teachers remember this in the classroom. The powers that be would be well advised to avoid using red in prisons or psychiatric units.)

Red carpets on a staircase are not a good idea as the red activates Chi – that plus the up and down motion could be very disquieting.

YANG   RED   ORANGE
紅   橙

Red is good in the South, Southwest, and Northeast.

Brown is practical and down-to-earth (literally). It is good in the Northeast – the knowledge section – and the Southwest.

Orange represents gathering and is good as a highlight in creative/social environments. Good for health and vitality. It is good in the Southwest and Northeast.

Yellow (earth element) represents authority – it is invigorating and stimulates mental energy and tolerance – good for the intellect and concentration, so use it in an office. Yellow is good in the Southwest, Northeast, Northwest, and West.

Many successful companies use red and yellow in their logos. This combines the dynamic force of the red and gathering qualities of yellow.

Green (wood element) represents longevity and peace.

Pastel green is good in the boardroom as this stimulates a sense of growth within a company (associated with the rising energy of a tree). It represents harmony and receptiveness – don't use too much though as it could make you feel ungrounded.

Blue (navy) represents heaven's blessings – it is a very calming color and is good for a business where communication is a priority. It reflects a sense of reliable honesty. In a bedroom it is calming (use a warm soft blue).

Green, turquoise, and blue are associated with wood energy – 3 (East) and 4 (Southeast). These colors are good in the South (see the supportive cycle on page 150).

Pink belongs to the fire element and is feminine. It also has healing qualities. Use it in the relationship section (Southwest).

Violet may be too passive in an office and could create drowsiness. It is good if tranquility is required.

Purple is a fire element and the color of the philosopher – it is good if used in the South (9 – fame) and Northeast (8 – knowledge). Good for a meditation room.

When using colors, apply the principles of Yin–Yang balance and focus on the elements you wish or need to enhance. The spectrum goes from Yang to Yin. Red (fire) creates Yang energy ... while black/blue (water) creates Yin energy.

The colors of the supportive cycle are good together (see page 150): red–yellow; yellow–white; white–black; black–green; green–red.

Be aware of the color that nourishes your Basic Nature Number and that of significant others in the environment.

Gold and silver represent the elements of metal in the West and Northwest. Gold is often used in China with red, they believe this brings luck and wealth.

YELLOW　　GREEN　BLUE　INDIGO　VIOLET　YIN

黄　　青　　藍　　靛藍　　紫

IF THE DIRECTION OF YOUR FRONT DOOR IS NOT FAVORABLE, USE THE FOLLOWING TABLE TO DETERMINE A FAVORABLE COLOR.

IF YOUR KUA NUMBER IS:

ORIENTATION OF DOOR	1	2	3	4	5	6	7	8	9
NORTH	S	C White/Gold/Silver	S	S	C White/Gold/Silver	C Yellows/Orange/Brown	C Yellows/Orange/Brown	C White/Gold/Silver	S
NORTHEAST	C White/Gold/Silver	S	C Red/Purple	C Red/Purple	S	S	S	S	C Green/Pale blue Red/Purple
EAST	S	C Red/Purple	S	S	C Red/Purple	C Black/Navy	C Black/Navy	C Red/Purple	S
SOUTHEAST	S	C Red/Purple	S	S	C Red/Purple	C Black/Navy	C Black/Navy	C Red/Purple	S
SOUTH	S	C Yellows	S	S	C Yellows	C Yellows/Orange	C Yellows/Orange	C Yellows/Orange	S
SOUTHWEST	C White/Gold/Silver	S Purple	C Red/Purple	C Red/	S	S	S	S	C Green/Pale blue/Red/Purple
WEST	C Black/Navy	S	C Black/Navy	C Black/Navy	S	S	S	S	C Brown/Yellows/Orange
NORTHWEST	C Black/Navy	S	C Black/Navy	C Black/Navy	S	S	S	S	C Brown/Yellows/Orange

S = Supporting   **C** = Challenging so use recommended colors.

If the direction of your door is not favorable, paint it a recommended color or bring that color into the area immediately as you enter.

For example, your Kua Number is 2 and your door faces Southeast, paint the door red or bring red into the hall somehow, such as with objects or a painted surface (see mitigating cycle, page 154).

COLOUR IS VERY POWERFUL ... USE IT CONSCIOUSLY

USING MIRRORS

Mirrors are very powerful. They draw in energy – expand it and then reflect it back – this encourages the movement of Chi through a building.

We have an energy field of vibration – an "aura" – around our physical body and frequently our mirrors are too small to reflect the whole field of energy that we radiate. Reflecting in a small mirror each morning or evening limits our sense of who we are.

The mirror we use to dress should reflect our full form. So ensure that they are hung at the right height. If they are too high you may feel ungrounded – if too low, they can create headaches.

All mirrors must be kept clean. A dirty mirror may bring in grubby energy – in the relationship section, this could bring a messy relationship. For the same reason do not use cracked or damaged mirrors. Cracked antique mirrors can be placed where they are not used for dressing. Tinted decorative mirrors should be avoided for dressing as you may see yourself in a "haze."

It is fine to see a mirror from your bed, but you should not be able to see your body reflected in it when lying down – this reflection will cause an expansion of vibration resulting in a more shallow sleep state. Sleep is for gathering Chi – if you are reflected in a mirror, Chi is expanded and dispersed.

Mirrors in the bedroom should be round or oval.

Mirrored sliding doors on a wardrobe or the front of a medicine cabinet are staggered so they reflect images from different depths – thus seeing yourself as divided. This can cause you to feel split.

Small mirrored tiles break images into hundreds of pieces so these are not good for reflecting in, but are fine as a decorative effect.

Mirrors can be used to transform negative space by creating the illusion of a full rectangle or square in an L- or U-shaped room – transcending an image into the absent space (see negative space on page 152).

PLANTS AND FLOWERS

Plants symbolize life and growth, increasing the oxygen in the environment – as a living organism they enhance Yin-Yang balance – remember to water them.

Plants in an office are potent as they emanate positive Chi and absorb negative Chi. They are particularly good in the Southeast, East and South.

Fresh flowers emanate vital Chi, but be aware that when they start to wither, their Chi is less nurturing – so replace them as necessary.

When colors fade, the energy fades. Bright colors raise our energy so in an internal environment use silk plants. Do not use dried flowers – these have had the life taken out of them.

Fresh flowers on your desk stimulate creativity.

Do not put fresh flowers or plants in your bedroom, too much Chi is activated, so they are not good for resting. This is different in a hospital, though, as the Yang Chi is balanced by the Yin environment.

If your office or home is below ground, use plants and shrubs to counter any heavy or depressing energy. Create some brightness in the lightwell by using colors.

Avoid prickly plants such as cacti – used externally they represent protection for the home, but internally they can feel attacking. Succulent, round-leafed plants are preferred. Bonsai plants, though beautiful, represent stunted growth so unless they are an absolute "must" avoid them.

If you have a spiral staircase, put potted plants underneath it to still the spiralling Chi.

Use plants to deflect the cutting Chi that projecting corners can create (see page 136).

If you were born in a wood year, plants are especially good for you to have around. Conversely, earth people should use plants in moderation.

ADVICE REGARDING CLUTTER

STORAGE IS DIFFERENT FROM CLUTTER.

Energy must be free to flow without obstruction. Check out where you have clutter and ask yourself if you want to block this area of your life. Sometimes clutter is created as a subconscious obstacle – blocking your potential success.

Clutter by a door blocks your approach to the world, especially if it faces South.

Clutter in the North – the tendency is to hide your feelings from others.

Clutter in the East or Southeast – the tendency is to be confused and indecisive. In the East this can additionally cause disharmony at home and you can have difficulty getting started.

Clutter in the Southwest – there is a tendency to become troubled in affairs of the heart.

Clutter in the West – you have difficulty in getting projects off the ground.

Clutter in the Northeast – problem with retaining information.

Clutter in the Northwest – tendency to be more controlling.

Clutter in the center – affects every area as this touches all the other numbers.

Do not ignore clutter in attics (representing your future) or basement (your past).

Clutter throughout your environment creates too much worry.

Just look where the clutter is in your office or home. It would be interesting to see, for example, if the clutter is in the relationship corner (Southwest) and that relationships in the office are difficult or there is difficulty in emotional relationships at home.

Clear the clutter.

Change clutter into organized systems. Discard what is not necessary and organize what is left. If it is information or data that can be computerized, do so, but clear out the rest.

Clutter on shelves overhead can create anxiety, a feeling of pressure on top of you. Instead of giving yourself a hard time about the clutter, just clear it.

Enjoy the clarity that comes with releasing blocked energy.

CLARITY LETS INTUITION COME THROUGH

CLEAR OUT THE CLUTTER

START WITH THE PHYSICAL

MOVE TO THE MENTAL

AND ON TO THE EMOTIONAL
WHEN YOU ARE READY

SO THAT INTUITION

DOES NOT HAVE TO SHOW UP AS HINDSIGHT

WIND CHIMES

The purpose of wind chimes is to moderate Chi, not to activate it. They can be used internally and externally.

Make sure that your wind chimes have hollow tubes.

If the front door is exactly opposite and in line with the back door, use a wind chime at the back door to prevent the Chi entering through the front door and going straight out the back.

Healthy Chi is attracted by movement and sound, so hang wind chimes at home if you are out at work all day.

Chimes are good at defining different areas – the air current creates a sound wave defining movement from one area to another.

Choose chimes carefully for their sweet sound and clarity – sound waves resonate differently for each of us.

If there are a number of doors in a row, use a wind chime to moderate the flow of Chi.

Too many windows can create chaotic Chi – a wind chime will still this flow.

Placing a wind chime at your front door enhances the energy entering your building – especially if the direction is not a supportive one for you.

Do not hang a wind chime above your bed or desk as this expansion of Chi could disturb your sleep and/or concentration respectively.

If your staircase directly aligns with your front door, place a wind chime near the inside of your door to prevent the Chi rushing out. Additionally, place a reflective disk on the inside of your door to reflect the energy back into the building.

Metal chimes are good in the West and Northwest (metal element).

Bamboo wind chimes are best in the East and Southeast (wood element). They can also be hung in the South sector, as its element is fire and wood feeds fire.

Pottery chimes belong in the Northeast, Southwest, Northwest, and West.

CRYSTALS

Crystals (earth element) have an extraordinary capacity to absorb – expand – and intensify Chi (be cautious about putting them on the computer). There are two distinct categories of crystal, both of which can be used. These are uncut mineral crystals, such as amethyst and rose quartz, or clear faceted lead crystals. As the sunlight passes through the faceted lead crystal, it refracts the light, splitting it into its full spectrum of colors – this expands Chi.

Choose crystals that are symmetrical.

Keep crystals clean by rinsing them in water (do not use salt water as this can damage the crystal).

Place a mineral crystal by your front door if it faces Southwest or Northeast (earth).

In some cases where there is a negative space and a window prevents the installation of a mirror, hang a lead cut crystal in the center of the wall to activate Chi. Sparkling objects of this type on a wall can be an effective cure as they expand the Chi.

Generally, if there are no windows, hang a lead cut crystal against a wall to enhance the Chi.

CLEANSING A BUILDING

Just as our mind sometimes needs an airing – through exercising, vacationing, or meditating – our environment needs a clearing too.

Over time, a building, its walls, floors, and furniture absorb different energies, and the atmosphere within the building can become energetically polluted. You have heard the expression when people have had an argument that "you could cut the atmosphere with a knife." To cleanse a building, sprinkle sea salt around the perimeter, walking clockwise or counterclockwise starting at your front door, especially across external thresholds and into corners (sea salt purifies by absorbing negative Chi). Then walk in a clockwise or counterclockwise direction around the perimeter of your building again, this time ringing a wind chime gently with the intent that its resonance will break up any stagnant Chi (give extra attention to the corners where energy often gets trapped).

Repeat this exercise on every level of the building, starting at the main door and then return to your starting point – completing the circle (women are advised not to do this if they are pregnant or menstruating as at these times they are more sensitive to energetic changes).

Do this ritual with the chimes three times (rinse the wind chimes between each of these). On the third cycle, imagine the resonance filling the room with harmonious, supportive Chi.

Before the process, clear as much clutter as possible, light a candle, and have some frankincense burning by a bowl of water on a table (pour the water out afterwards). Remove all jewelry during the process and preferably have bare feet or just wear socks or slippers.

Bathe afterwards – literal and symbolic cleansing. (Sea salt in your bath water will similarly cleanse **you**.)

THE ENVIRONMENT

Our environments are alive with the invisible forces of Yin and Yang and auspicious Chi is created when these are in balance. This Yin–Yang balance is effected by the landscape and the shape, size, materials, and colors of the structures built on it.

What shape is your building?

What kind of buildings are located nearby?

How is your building placed on the landscape – top of hill, bottom of hill?

Look at the neighboring buildings, roads and waterways.

Is your building overshadowed by larger structures?

Do you have your preferred locations and directions within the building?

Is there open space in front of your building where good Chi can gather to enter your building?

Is there water nearby – and if so what kind?

What is the history of the building – what happened to the previous tenants (see Predecessor Law on page 103)?

If the site is not a regular shape, look at the site from all angles – check its gradients and curves. Apply the concept of balance, and find creative solutions. Lights can counterbalance steep gradients by directing them upwards from the base of the slope. Lighting can also create an artificial boundary if set into the landscape of an L-shaped building.

Ideally, you want an undulating landscape – and as you exit your building, you want higher land to the left and lower land to the right. In Form School Feng Shui, the higher land represents the celestial Green Dragon and the lower land, the White Tiger. Where the high land (Green Dragon) meets the lower land (White Tiger) is considered the most auspicious place. Ideally, the Red Phoenix at the front should be lower than the Black Turtle at the back (see page 34).

Hills, mountains, and tall trees represent Yang energy. Valleys, rivers, and low flat land represent Yin energy.

In urban settings, the varying architectural proportions of buildings can be balanced by careful landscaping.

Today, large buildings represent the symbol of mountain (8 in the grid) and roads represent the symbol of rivers (1 in the grid).

CHI

Like the existence of opposites, in all things there is positive Chi and negative Chi.

Actually Chi is present in three phases:
Sheng Chi – vital, positive Chi.
Si Chi – waning Chi.
Sha Chi – negative or cutting Chi.

As Chi passes a sharp corner it begins to spin, forming eddies like on the bend of a fast-flowing river. This energy spin is called Cutting Chi and can happen inside or outside a building. If you sit within the field of Cutting Chi, you could feel disorientated. In a room, placement of plants can disperse this Cutting Chi.

Open spaces allow Sheng Chi to gather so this would be good near your entrance. To avoid the Cutting Chi that comes from a T-junction in an urban setting – plant bushes and shrubs as a barrier, or put something reflective at the front of the building to deflect it away. Be aware of Cutting Chi from rooftops or the corners of buildings pointing directly at the windows of your apartment or office. You can use a convex mirror to deflect and disperse this.

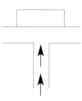

The driveways and paths to a building should be wider at the street end and narrower closer to the building. This encourages the energy to come into the building. It helps if the path meanders in gentle curves, preventing cutting Chi from hitting the entrance.

If the road slopes gently down toward your building – this is luck pouring in.

Driveways that slope downward away from your door drain Chi away. Direct a light upward from the bottom of the slope.

Avoid homes and offices that overlook flyovers because of the Cutting Chi. If you are already occupying one in this kind of location then use a cure, such as a convex mirror, to deflect these arrows of Cutting Chi.

Straight roads create Cutting Chi, winding roads create positive (Sheng) Chi.

WATER

Chi tends to accumulate around areas of water, so water is regarded as auspicious.

It is especially auspicious for people of the water and wood elements. The sound of running water is very soothing.

The energy of moving water is more Yang than that of still water (Yin). A fresh water lake is more Yin, so ... living by a lake is more peaceful than living by a river.

A waterfall is Yang and salt water from the sea is Yang.

A meandering stream which gives Chi a chance to settle is preferred to a fast flowing river.

Water flowing toward your front door brings vitality and money ... water flowing away from your entrance can carry that vitality away.

A waterfall or fountain in the Southeast of a garden is very good, i.e. water (1) feeding wealth (4).

HILLS

It is considered auspicious to have a hill at the back of your home (the Black Turtle). In the city, the equivalent is having a high-rise building or tall trees.

Sharp rocky mountains are considered more Yang – and are represented by the fire element. Round rolling hills are more Yin and are represented by the metal element.

On a hill, you preferably want the Yang sunny side, which increases your exposure to the sun's energy. The Chi of your building may be more stagnant if it is in the shade.

The closer you are to the top of a mountain, the more you will be influenced by Yang (active) energy. The closer you are to the bottom of the slope – you will be more influenced by Yin, as here the Chi moves more slowly. A location halfway up produces the most advantageous balance.

QUALITIES OF DIRECTION AND LOCATION

The differing orientations of your door brings in different luck – so apart from the directions that support your personal Kua number, generally a door facing:

北

NORTH	brings business success.
NORTHEAST	is good for scholars but not so good for business, as it supports questions rather than answers.
EAST	enhances family unity.
SOUTHEAST	brings wealth and prosperity.
SOUTH	attracts a good reputation.
SOUTHWEST	attracts a good relationship.
WEST	helps the children of the household.
NORTHWEST	is good for people who travel a lot – or wish to.

西 東

General locations within your home

NORTH	bedrooms, relaxation room, storage, garage.
NORTHEAST	games room, storeroom.
EAST	kitchen, study (office), dining room, children's playroom, bedroom.
SOUTHEAST	dining room, study (office), kitchen.
SOUTH	living room, study.
SOUTHWEST	living room, master bedroom.
WEST	dining room, bedroom, child's bedroom.
NORTHWEST	study, dining room, master bedroom.

南

A HOUSE BENEFITS FROM THE ENERGY OF A PET

Dogs   Dogs belong to the earth element, so let its blanket or basket be an earth color, such as beige or yellow.

Cats   These belong to the wood element and are thought to ward off negative energy. It is a curious fact that cats tend to sit where there is negative Chi. Check out where this is in your home and sprinkle some sea salt in that area. This absorbs the negative Chi and does the cat no harm.

Rabbits   These are good in the relationship corner as they represent happy relationships, being symbolic of love and warmth.

Fish   In the Orient fish represent abundance, so if this resonates with you put them in the Southeast section (wealth area) in large oxygenated, clean aquariums. (The Chinese word for fish sounds like the word for success.)

Birds   These are associated with the earth element. Placing some stones at the base of their large cage is good. A birdbath in the garden can attract vital Chi.

Tortoises   They belong to the turtle family and are considered very auspicious – they represent the earth element.

Horses   They represent the fire element and supposedly endow their owner with power.

Frogs   As a symbol, a frog is purported to bring wealth (gold and silver) into your life. In China they place them inside the home, near the front door.

Animal figures as charms are popular in China, especially lions, tigers, dragons, and turtles (tortoises).

NUMBERS HAVE THEIR OWN VIBRATIONS

In the Chinese system, they add together the number of strokes it takes to write each number or digit.

F E N G S H U I
3 4 3 2 1 3 1 1
3+ 4+ 3+ 2+ 1+ 3+ 1+ 1 = **18**

Refer to numbers 1 and 8 in the chart opposite (the Chinese consider 8 a very auspicious number).

In the Western system, the letters are assigned numbers as follows:

A B C D E F G H I
J K L M N O P Q R
S T U V W X Y Z
1 2 3 4 5 6 7 8 9

So, the words Feng Shui work out as:

F E N G S H U I
6 5 5 7 1 8 3 9
6+ 5+ 5+ 7+ 1+ 8+ 3+ 9 = **44**

In this system there is only one ruling number so 44 is reduced to a single digit:

44 = 4+4 = **8**

Refer to number 8 in the chart opposite.

As illustrated above, this ruling number is ascertained by adding up all the numbers and if the resulting number has more than one digit these are added together until one single number remains.

eg **T H E   H A T   S H O P**
    2 8 5   8 1 2   1 8 6 7
    2+ 8+ 5 + 8+ 1+ 2 + 1+ 8+ 6+ 7 = **48**
                 48:    4+ 8 = **12**
                 12:    1+ 2 = **3**

Refer to number 3 in the chart opposite.

If the number of your house is 6, you can create the energy of a 7 house by changing it to 6a.
A = **1**
6+A = 6+1 = **7**

QUALITIES OF NUMBERS

1 Good for health and independence – be ca[reful] not to isolate yourself here.

2 You could become a bit too dependent but your compassion will grow. Hang a metal wind chime at the front door to exhaust some of the earth element.

3 A lot of communication and social activity here. Be cautious of becoming overconfident and too impulsive.

4 The people here will tend to work hard. It is a place of balance and can bring security, including financial.

5 Here the occupants, like number 5 itself in the grid, are at the center of things. The energy is very strong. To harness this supportively, check your Feng Shui and hang a metal wind chime to exhaust more of the earth element.

6 The occupants here tend to be very social, and this house is a good place to raise a family. Make an effort to be sensible with your savings. Although this number's colors are gold and silver, which represent [rich]es, caution is advised so that it does not become fad[ing] prosperity.

7 Seven [is a] mystical number and represents heaven's wisdom. [It is a] very good house for study and for raising childre[n. M]oney-wise it is lucky.

8 Great knowledge a[nd] good luck comes to you here, but take care not to [be]come too materialistic.

9 A very auspicious num[ber], it brings prosperity into your future. Here you ca[n en]hance your reputation – and even gain recognition.

You may have heard that the Chinese avoid the number 4. The reason for this is because in Cant[on]e[se] it sounds like the word for death. Similarly, number 2 is considered unlucky because in Mandarin it sounds like the word for kill. Obviously these concerns do not apply to our Western culture.

The Chinese believe in cycles of time – each cycle lasting 180 years and the periods with[in each] lasting 20 years (the 9 numbers of the Lo Shu grid x 20 years = 180 years).

In each period of time there is a reigning number. The number reigning in the curr[ent p]eriod of 20 years is 7 (a particularly auspicious number) and this will be so until 2003 – the fo[llow]ing period of 20 years will have the reigning number 8.

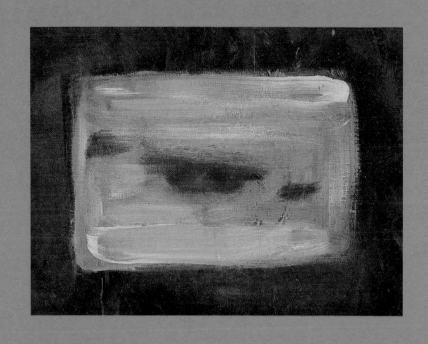

EVERYTHING YOU HAVE READ SO FAR IS ONLY THE TIP

OF THE PROVERBIAL ICEBERG

KNOWING THE ICEBERG IS THERE

CAN MAKE ALL THE DIFFERENCE

EINSTEIN TOOK A QUANTUM LEAP BEYOND THE KNOWN

SCIENCE NOW CONCURS

I HOPE ONE DAY

WE WILL ALL HEAR THE SOUND OF

THE CHINESE WHISPERS

天體

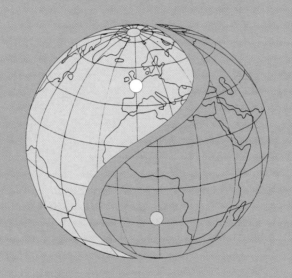

This is a three-dimensional subject and the foundation of your understanding, like the foundations of a building, needs to be solid before you move onward.

Here is some more in-depth theory behind the principles of Feng Shui.

THE ELEMENT CYCLES

COMPATIBILITY OF THE ELEMENTS

USING THE CURES AND SYMBOLS TO COUNTERACT ANY IMBALANCES

SOUTHERN HEMISPHERE

THE ELEMENT CYCLES

THE FIVE ELEMENTS RELATE TO EACH OTHER ACCORDING TO THE FOLLOWING CYCLES: THE NATURAL CYCLE (USING ITS OWN ELEMENTS) – THE CREATIVE/SUPPORTIVE CYCLE – THE EXHAUSTIVE CYCLE – THE DESTRUCTIVE CYCLE – AND THE MITIGATING CYCLE.

SUPPORTIVE CYCLE

THE CREATIVE/SUPPORTIVE CYCLE OF THE ELEMENTS

Here Chi moves in a clockwise motion.

Fire creates **earth** (ash); Under pressure **earth** hardens into **metal** (minerals);

Metal under pressure melts and creates liquid – **water** – through condensation;

Water feeds **wood** (plants); **Wood** helps the **fire** to burn.

DESTRUCTIVE CYCLE

THE DESTRUCTIVE CYCLE OF THE ELEMENTS

Since life always has its opposite – following the star formation you can see the arrows of destruction.

Fire melts **metal**; **Metal** cuts **wood**; **Wood** (roots) spreads **earth**;

Earth clogs **water**; **Water** puts out the **fire**.

EXHAUSTIVE CYCLE

THE EXHAUSTIVE CYCLE OF THE ELEMENTS

(when the flow is counterclockwise)

Too much **fire** burns up all the **wood**; Too much **wood** drinks all the **water**;

Excess **water** rusts the **metal**; **Metal** diminishes **earth** to rock;

Too much **earth** (ash) puts out the **fire**.

MITIGATING CYCLE

THE MITIGATING CYCLE OF THE ELEMENTS

The mitigating element is the one between the destructive cycle.

Earth mitigates **fire** and **metal**; **Metal** mitigates **water** and **earth**;

Water mitigates **wood** and **metal**; **Wood** mitigates **fire** and **water**;

Fire mitigates **wood** and **earth**.

WOOD   Represents all living things. Its nature is an upward movement of energy
         and it is associated with the rising energy of springtime.

FIRE   Its nature is upward and outward, symbolizing expansion, burning, and heat.
         It is associated with the active energy of summer.

EARTH   Its nature is downward and grounding and it is associated with the settling energy
         of late summer.

METAL   Symbolizes condensing, inward, consolidating energy and it is associated with
         the harvest time of autumn.

WATER   This is the part of the cycle where the energy is floating and appears dormant.
         It is associated with the stillness of winter.

THE STAR CYCLE
THIS CAN BE USED TO DETERMINE COMPATIBILITY OF THE NUMBERS

The numbers within the same element share great commonality and understand each other
(natural cycle). Adjacent numbers are very compatible and in romance share great passion.

For example, number 4 has great passion and friendship with number 9. Numbers 6 and 7
can share great friendship and even lasting intimacy, though not perhaps with the same passion
as adjacent numbers.

With the numbers opposite each other, there is more difficulty (follow the arrows on the
destructive cycle).

So, use the cures (see next page) to combat personal difficulty.

For example, a number 8 person has to be very careful with a number 3 person. They may be too
different. If they have to live together or work together, bring in something representing 9
(mitigating cycle).

Numbers 5 and 1:
Number 1 loses clarity, so this is not a good mix. Use the mitigating cycle and introduce a 6 or 7
person or images thereof.

Water (1) puts out fire (9) (destructive cycle) – so a number 1 finds it hard to be best of friends
with a 9. Mitigate with a 3 or 4 by using plants and the colors green or pale blue in the
environment at work or at home.

GUIDE TO USING THE CYCLES FOR COLORS IN YOUR ENVIRONMENT

Number in Lo Shu grid	Represents	Natural cycle	Creative/supportive cycle	Destructive cycle
1	Career	Navy, black	White, gold, silver, gray	Yellow, ocher, orange, brown
2	Relationship	Yellow, ocher	Red, purple	Green, pale blue
3	Ancestors (roots)	Green, pale blue	Navy, black	White, gold, silver, gray
4	Wealth	Green, pale blue	Navy, black	White, gold, silver, gray
5	Chi	Yellow, ocher, orange	Red, purple	Green, pale blue
6	Helpful friends	White, gold, silver, gray	Yellow, ocher, brown, orange	Red, purple
7	Creativity	White, gold, silver, gray	Yellow, ocher, brown, orange	Red, purple
8	Knowledge	Orange, brown, ocher	Red, purple	Green, pale blue
9	Fame	Red, purple	Green, pale blue	Navy, black

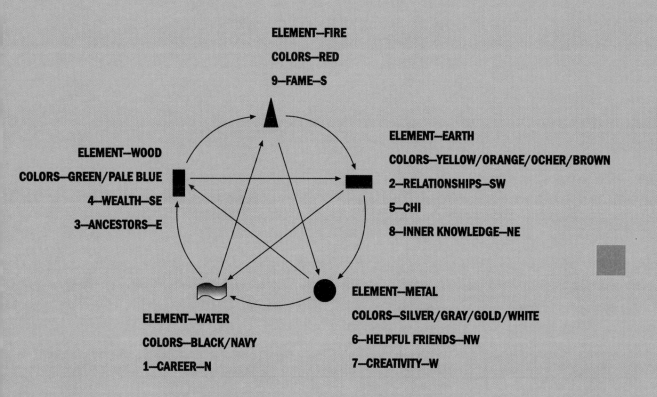

ELEMENT—FIRE
COLORS—RED
9—FAME—S

ELEMENT—EARTH
COLORS—YELLOW/ORANGE/OCHER/BROWN
2—RELATIONSHIPS—SW
5—CHI
8—INNER KNOWLEDGE—NE

ELEMENT—WOOD
COLORS—GREEN/PALE BLUE
4—WEALTH—SE
3—ANCESTORS—E

ELEMENT—METAL
COLORS—SILVER/GRAY/GOLD/WHITE
6—HELPFUL FRIENDS—NW
7—CREATIVITY—W

ELEMENT—WATER
COLORS—BLACK/NAVY
1—CAREER—N

CURES

It is rare to find an existing environment that is perfect. So the cycles and the following Feng Shui cures are used to enhance and create balance. These cures are used by applying them to the relevant sections of the grid. Each numbered section of the grid is represented by a shape, a symbol, an image, seasons, times of the day, anatomy, family members, and much more.

Number in Lo Shu grid	Compass orientation	Element	Shape	Color (natural cycle)	Time of day	Symbolic representation[1]	Area of life
1	NORTH	WATER	ASYMMETRICAL WAVY	BLACK/NAVY	NIGHT	Images of moving water. You don't want stillness here, rather images of what you would love to do: sailing – skiing – waterfalls – aquarium – glass – seascapes – paints – mirrors	Career – freedom to do what you want – your journey in life
2	SOUTHWEST	EARTH	SQUARE/FLAT RECTANGLE	YELLOWS/OCHER	AFTERNOON	Images of union – no images of solitary figures here – photographs of union – crystals – cushions – ceramics – flowers – two candles – pairs of things	Relationship – platonic, romantic, professional
3	EAST	WOOD	RECTANGLE SQUARE	GREEN/PALE BL	MORNING	Images of rising energy – sunrise – tall plants. This represents thunder so music, stereo, piano, television. Wood element – bamboo – family photographs	Ancestors – superiors and parents – authority figures
4	SOUTHEAST	WOOD	RECTANGLE SQUARE	GREEN/PALE BL	LATE MORNING	Images of rising energy – tall plants. This represents wind – stereo – piano – television. Wood element – bamboo – family photograph – ceramics – gold coins – waterfall – mobile – fans	Wealth and blessings
5	CENTER	EARTH	SQUARE/FLAT RECTANGLE	YELLOW/OCHER ORANGE	FEMALE— AFTERNOON MALE— LATE MORNING	Water in this area should be clean and flowing – crystals – ceramic pots	Chi – health
6	NORTHWEST	STRONG METAL	ROUND/OVAL	SILVER/GOLD/ WHITE/GRAY	DUSK	Images of support (teachers – gurus) – metal wind chimes	Helpful friends – neighbors, staff, mentors, supporters
7	WEST	LITTLE METAL	ROUND/OVAL	SILVER/GOLD/ WHITE/GRAY	EARLY EVENING	Images of playfulness – children's paintings – sunsets – animals – vase of white flowers – ornaments – lakes – games – metal wind chimes	Creativity – joy, inspiration, children
8	NORTHEAST	EARTH	SQUARE/FLAT RECTANGLE	YELLOWS/ ORANGE/OCHER/ BROWN	EARLY MORNING	Images of heavy cabinets (represents mountains) – chests – empty boxes – cupboards/drawers – crystal	Inner knowledge – wisdom
9	SOUTH	FIRE	TRIANGULAR	RED/PURPLE	MIDDAY	Inspirational images – lights – candles – images of heroes or ambitions – or dreams – painting/sculptures	Fame – illumination in the world

1 Some of these representations have their origins in the East – these can be substituted with Western images of good luck. For example a metal horseshoe could be used in the West sector, whereas in China they may use the image of a dragon, etc.

NEGATIVE AND POSITIVE SPACE

Due to an irregular shape in a room, home, or office there may be missing sections within the grid. These areas are called negative space.

For example, in Diagram A: sections 7 and 3 have NEGATIVE SPACE.

Where sections of the building extend beyond the grid, these areas are called POSITIVE SPACE.

For example, in Diagram B: section 6 has POSITIVE SPACE.
In Diagram C: sections 3 and 8 have NEGATIVE SPACE; 2 has POSITIVE SPACE.

Diagram A

N

1	8	3
6	5	4
7	2	9

Diagram B

3	4	9
8	5	2
1	6	7

N

Diagram C

4	9	2
3	5	7
8	1	6

N

Ways to compensate and balance Negative and Positive Spaces are given opposite.

Positive space is usually beneficial.

Missing space in 5 is like having an internal courtyard. Many traditional cultures have this and it is an excellent feature. Clean running water in this area is good – not a pond though, as still water pollutes easily (5 is the health area).

To set your grid correctly on an irregular shaped site, position it so that the individual negative and positive spaces do not exceed 15% of the total site area.

THIS IS WHAT HAPPENS IN YOUR LIFE IF YOU HAVE NEGATIVE AND POSITIVE SPACE IN A BUILDING OR ROOM

Location	Result of negative space in this area	Result of positive space in this area
North	Difficult for career. Creates weakness and depression. Blocks thought – leads to confusion. Introduce water images.	Clear about ambitions. Career blossoms, particularly good for women. Excess positive space creates isolation and possible loneliness.
Northeast	Feel unstable and forgetful. Not good for scholars.	Knowledge grows, but there can be disagreements. Encourages greediness, boredom, and insomnia.
East	Misunderstanding, some ill-health and loss of vitality.	Sense of maturity and success for the occupants. Excess positive space creates hyperactivity – could become over-ambitious and careless.
Southeast	Income affected. Difficulties in business. Confusion. Accidents.	Prosperity and success. Excess positive space – over-sensitive and tired.
South	Become self-conscious, lose confidence, lose reputation. Lack of clarity.	Expect promotion and recognition. Excess positive space here creates conceit, could become notorious – tendency to emotional swings.
Southwest	Feel unstable, hard to find a relationship. Difficult for women.	Particularly good for women here and encourages romance. Excess positive space here – you could become slow and get in a rut – becoming overdependent.
West	Difficulty around children, loss of joy, hard to save money, emotional blocks.	Helps completion of projects – very sociable and happy. Excess positive space – obsession with pleasure and tendency to greediness.
Northwest	Not many helpers, lack of vitality. Difficult for men. Children can be disobedient. Introduce metal or earth.	Concern for others grows and good financially – stimulates clear judgement. Excess positive space – overcontrolling and a bit self-righteous.

When numbered sections are missing (Negative Space), use the element of the natural or creative/supportive cycle to restore balance (cures).

If you have negative space in 1 (career), use 6 and 7 from the supportive cycle – bring extra metal or the color white – gold – silver into the rest of the decor of the building. If possible, use a mirror on the wall of the absent career section and transcend into that space. Have images of the water element (and its other representations from the natural cycle) in career sections of other rooms in the building.

USING THE SUPPORTIVE CYCLE

If you want to stimulate wealth (4) in your life, activate the Southeast section (4) using the supportive cycle – introduce the water elements – water's colors are black and navy.

USING THE EXHAUSTIVE CYCLE

If excitement and fire (9) energy is too strong, use earth (2, 5, 8) element and colors to subdue.

USING THE DESTRUCTIVE CYCLE

If there is far too much fire energy, let's say the room is red, and you are a number 6 (therefore you are being melted), bring in a cure representing number 1 (water) and put out the fire. A picture of a waterfall to destroy the fire would help or stone sculptures to exhaust and subdue it.

Fire people (9) would benefit from a South position (9) (natural cycle) and should generally avoid water (1) and the colors black and navy – this is the destructive cycle. Remember that we want balance in all things, so we want some water – some earth – metal – wood – fire – but not excess of one, especially if it is the element that undermines your basic nature or your kind of business.

USING THE MITIGATING CYCLE

Use the mitigating cycle to encourage balance where opposites exist. This refers to conflict of elements, colors, symbols, and people.

If the business is finance (4) (represents wealth) and the environment has lots of metal (6) (steel chairs and cabinets), bring in water (1) – the color black or navy, or an image of a waterfall. (Avoid using representations of earth [2, 5 or 8] as this clogs water and invigorates metal.)

If water element (1) is too strong (too emotional, too much black or navy and you are a fire person), use wood (3, 4) in the form of, for example, green plants to exhaust water and support fire.

If a person whose Kua Number is 6 has to work with a 3, bring in a 1 to work there or images of 1 (see mitigating cycle on page 148).

If your Kua Number is 1 and the room you work is in the Southwest (2), and the color is yellow and there is a stone floor (earth), bring in metal (6, 7) (tables and chairs, etc.) to enhance your environment.

If your Kua Number is 9 and your door faces West (7), paint the door yellow (2) (see color on page 124).

If the direction of your door is not supportive, use the mitigating cycle to ascertain mutually supportive colors and paint your door that color.

YOUR KUA NUMBER REPRESENTS AN ELEMENT ON THE STAR CYCLE AND THIS MAY DIFFER FROM THE ELEMENT OF YOUR YEAR OF BIRTH.

For example, a woman born on September 9, 1953 – ELEMENT of YEAR is WATER, element of her KUA NUMBER 4 is WOOD – so she is influenced by both WOOD and WATER.

A man born on March 8, 1948 – ELEMENT of YEAR is EARTH element of his KUA NUMBER 8 is EARTH – so he is doubly influenced by EARTH CHARACTERISTICS.

A woman born on April 4,1967 – ELEMENT of YEAR is FIRE, element of her KUA NUMBER 9 is FIRE – so she is doubly influenced by FIRE CHARACTERISTICS – WATCH OUT NUMBER 7s.

A man born on July 27, 1961 – ELEMENT of YEAR is METAL, element of his KUA NUMBER 3 is WOOD – so he is influenced by WOOD and METAL.

風水

THE CHINESE ANIMAL SIGNS ARE ASSOCIATED WITH THE

FOLLOWING WESTERN ASTROLOGICAL SIGNS

RAT – Sagittarius   HORSE – Gemini
OX – Capricorn   SHEEP – Cancer
TIGER – Aquarius   MONKEY – Leo
RABBIT – Pisces   ROOSTER – Virgo
DRAGON – Aries   DOG – Libra
SNAKE – Taurus   PIG – Scorpio

Feng Shui enhancements are generally worked through symbolism – derived from their associated Trigram. If you wish to understand this at a deeper level, read a translation of the *I Ching*.

THE TRIGRAMS AND THE SOUTHERN HEMISPHERE

There is a small body of people evolving a new school of thought that questions the efficacy of maintaining the original Trigram positions for the Southern Hemisphere.

The sun sits to the North of the Tropic of Capricorn so in the Southern Hemisphere (South of the Tropics) the sun shines in the North – therefore they suggest that Trigram Li – 離 – South – fire – 9 – should switch with Trigram K'an – 坎 – North – water – 1.

選擇

IF THE CHOICE CONFUSES YOU, SET UP A TEST USING THE TRADITIONAL METHOD OF ORIENTATION INITIALLY AND THEN THE OTHER – JUDGE FOR YOURSELF.

If you choose to apply this new theory then you will need to apply the following changes to the section on personality analysis on page 66. With this new perspective, your season of birth changes as spring now becomes autumn and summer becomes winter, in the Southern Hemisphere – so your personality number will adjust to suit. The dates in the right hand-column below are for the Southern Hemisphere, to enable you to convert your season for the chart on page 66.

February 4–March 5	Spring	August 8–September 7
March 6–April 4	Spring	September 8–October 8
April 5–May 5	Spring	October 9–November 7
May 6–June 5	Summer	November 8–December 7
June 6–July 7	Summer	December 8–January 5
July 8–August 7	Summer	January 6–February 3
August 8–September 7	Autumn	February 4–March 5
September 8–October 8	Autumn	March 6–April 4
October 9–November 7	Autumn	April 5–May 5
November 8–December 7	Winter	May 6–June 5
December 8–January 5	Winter	June 6–July 7
January 6–February 3	Winter	July 8–August 7

BY APPLYING FENG SHUI THERE IS NOTHING TO BE LOST

AND EVERYTHING TO BE GAINED.

I hope you have enjoyed this journey from the East.

My wish is for buildings to enhance the lives
of the people they serve.

If we take care of how we create our buildings, our
buildings will take care of us – a synergy that
becomes more than the sum of the parts.

祝生

I WISH YOU JOY AND LUCK.

Rosalyn Dexter came to Feng Shui via a successful career

in property development and design. Realizing that she was

unconsciously using many of the principles of Feng Shui in her

most successful buildings, she developed her knowledge

of the subject and trained with many respected masters.

Rosalyn continues to work as a consultant in building

development, as well as carrying out Feng Shui consultations

for a range of high-profile personal and company clients.

IF YOU HAVE QUESTIONS OR SUGGESTIONS REGARDING THE
INFORMATION IN THIS BOOK PLEASE FORWARD THEM TO
PO BOX 21263, LONDON W9 1YU